Gann

by
Brian P. Fiddler

Series Editor
David Gibbings

First published 1990
Picton Publishing (Chippenham) Ltd.

Copyright 1988 Brian P. Fiddler
ISBN 0 948251 51 4

Typeset in 10 / 11 Times Roman
Printed in Great Britain by Picton Print
Ivy Road Industrial Estate, Chippenham, Wiltshire

(Cover) The Second Gannet AS2 Prototype, VR557, overflying a submarine during exercises.

I. I. Museum

An aerial view of the Fairey 17, VR546, later to become the prototype Gannet. Note the two-seat layout, lack of finlets and the Double Mamba propellers, in this instance at full power. It is interesting to note that even as late as 1949, the P marking denoting a prototype was still carried. This was introduced during the war (1941) to ensure that in the event of diversion or accident the aircraft would be properly guarded.

INTRODUCTION

The Gannet story encompasses virtually the whole of the post-war history of the Fleet Air Arm. Originally designed to counter the growing submarine threat, the Gannet eventually became the 'Eyes of the Fleet' through it's development into the essential airborne early warning role. The Gannet never achieved the public fame of the new generation of jet aircraft such as the Phantom and the Buccaneer but nevertheless performed a role that was just as vital and its demise is still regarded by many defence experts as being one of the major policy mistakes over the past two decades.

This book covers the full story of the Gannet's production and Royal Navy service, together with details of Squadrons, Shore Stations and Carriers in which the Gannet served. Details of Squadron Codes and representative aircraft are used only where documentary or photographic proof exists. The final chapter details the preserved Gannets around the United Kingdom where several examples are restored to their full Fleet Air Arm markings, particularly at the Fleet Air Arm Museum, Yeovilton and the Wales Aircraft Museum at Cardiff International Airport.

History is often said to be a collection of ironies and this is particularly true in the case of the Gannet Story. Having pioneered the use of airborne early warning at sea during the 1950's, the Royal Navy was deprived of a Gannet replacement in the infamous 1965 Defence Review, a mistake for which the Royal Navy was to pay dearly in the loss of ships and men in the Falklands Conflict. At the other end of the scale the millions of pounds expended upon the R.A.F.'s airborne early warning has, at the time of writing, resulted in just six Shackleton, piston-engined aircraft, themselves older than the Navy's Gannet AEW3's soldiering on until the introduction of the AWACS in the early 1990's. The Nimrod AEW tragedy is another story in itself, but the dead hand of political incompetence is the principal feature of both stories.

Governments rise and fall, and the recent Geneva Summit may yet produce a start to a Nuclear Free World. Nevertheless, the Royal Navy continues to face an increasing conventional threat and the Falklands Conflict displayed the necessity to maintain sufficient maritime forces to operate on a world-wide basis. The current threat is the Gulf, which poses questions on the Governments intended cuts in the Royal Navy's surface fleet and it is hoped that the lessons learned from the Gannets early demise will enable wiser counsels to prevail.

Photograph taken on the occasion of a Royal visit by H.M. The Queen, believed to be at RNAS Ford in 1953. This picture shows rather clearly the double set of variable pitch, contra-rotating propellers used to give greater fuel efficiency in flight.

2

THE ANTI-SUBMARINE GANNET

The story of the Gannet goes back as far as 1935, when Fairey's chief engine designer, Captain A. G. Forsyth, (later to achieve fame as their helicopter engineer) proposed the concept of the 'double' engine, later to become the Fairey P.24 Prince. The P.24 was a compact engine, designed to provide twin-engine capabilities without the problems of stowage and handling of large, twin-aircraft; an idea naturally of considerable advantage for carrier-borne operations. In the face of an economic recession and characteristic Government disinterest, Fairey persisted with their 'double' engine configuration and the P.24 proceeded with bench-runs, albeit with each half being tested separately. In early 1939, Fairey Battle K9370 was converted into a flying test-bed for the P.24. These tests met with such success that the P.24 was considered as a possible engine for both the Hawker Tornado and Typhoon, whilst the propellers of the P.24 were possibly the very first controllable-pitch, contra-rotating type in the world to be flight-tested.

The events of September 1939 overtook the test programme but the Americans became interested and the Battle was transferred to Wright Field, Ohio for evaluation. The Ford Motor Company intended to produce the P.24 for the Republic P.47 Thunderbolt, but after Pearl Harbour, all energy had to be concentrated upon existing designs and the Battle was returned to the Royal Aircraft Establishment at Farnborough.

Nevertheless the 'double-engined' concept was still considered as a viable proposition and the development of the Royal Navy's anti-submarine force after 1945 required a much greater cruising and patrol range. This led to the 'Twin-Merlin' project with two Rolls Royce Merlin engines mounted in tandem, dri ing independent co-axial 3-blade propellers. Fairey subsequently proposed to Armstrong-Siddeley, the idea of coupling together two Mamba propeller turbines. In 1945 design work c ommenced to produce the Double Mamba A5MD1 to power Fairey's bid for the Navy's two-seat anti-submarine strike aircraft (Spec GR17/45). The P24 'double-engine', as developed by Fairey, is now at the Fleet Air Arm Museum at Yeovilton.

Blackburn were also bidding for the new anti-submarine contract in the shape of the YB1 and Fairey developed the Fairey Type Q, designed by a team led by H.E. Chaplin (Chief Designer) and D.L. Hollis (Chief Engineer). This was initially to be powered by a Rolls Royce Tweed double-propeller turbine. Pressure of work, however, on other projects led to Rolls Royce terminating work upon the Tweed, whereby the Fairey Q, in effect the prototype of the Gannet, was ordered by the Ministry of Supply.

Three prototypes were built as follows:-

VR546:
Originally known as the Fairey GR17, this two-seat aircraft was the first Gannet prototype, making its first flight on 19th September 1949 with Group Captain Slade from Aldermaston at the controls, a Fulmar piloted by Peter Twiss acting as chase. On March 13th 1950, VR546 flew again with a third cockpit added, necessitating auxillary fins on the tailplane. The prototype became the first turbo-propeller aircraft to land on board a carrier when, on 19th June 1950, Lt. Cdr. G.R. Callingham landed

VR546 on board H.M.S. Illustrious. In May 1952 VR546 was transferred from Fairey's test-programme base at White Waltham to Boscombe Down for deck landing trials, culminating in a period aboard H.M.S. Eagle.

A further shot of prototype VR546, seen landing on board ILLUSTRIOUS on June 19, 1950, the first occasion of a turbo-propeller aircraft to land aboard a carrier.

A series of photographs showing the flight trials of the first Gannet prototype, VR546, from Aldermaston on 19 September 1949.

4

Air Survey Co.

Air Survey Co.

Air Survey Co.

6

Prototype VR546 displaying the Gannet's characteristic wing-folding technique.

VR557:
The second prototype, made its first flight on July 6th 1950.

WE488:
The third prototype was used as the production prototype Gannet, being similar in appearance to all subsequent production aircraft. Making its first flight on May 10th 1951, WE488 was damaged beyond repair in an accident at Turnhouse on October 9th 1953.

During the evaluation programme Fairey were awarded the contract and from 1955, the Gannet formed the core of the Fleet Air Arm's carrier-borne anti-submarine force. The Gannet was the first aircraft to operate with a double airscrew-turbine unit, giving all the advantages of a twin-engined aircraft within a single engine. Each half of the Double-Mamba engine could be controlled independently, with the other half being 'feathered', extending the cruising range and yet giving extra speed from both units during combat, both features of considerable advantage in anti-submarine warfare.

The Double-Mamba was designed to operate on kerosene or naval diesel fuel with the intention of eliminating petrol from Royal Navy carriers. The Gannet became the first Fleet Air Arm aircraft to combine the search and strike role and all its weapons, including two torpedoes, were stowed internally.

On March 14th 1951, the Gannet was ordered under the Governments 'Super

Air Survey Co.

A nice aerial view of 2nd AS1 prototype VR557, showing its retractable search equipment used for detecting submarines.

Priority Scheme' but delay in Gannets reaching squadron service led to 100 Grumman Avenger AS4's being made available under the Mutual Defence Aid Programme from the U.S.A. The Avengers comprised the Fleet Air Arms' anti-submarine force up to 1955 when Gannets started to be delivered to front-line squadrons.

The first version of the Gannet was the AS1, fitted with a Double Mamba (100) A5MDI engine and built at the Fairey plant at Hayes. Assembly of the AS1's took place at Northolt and delivery to the Fleet Air Arm was made at White Waltham. The first production Gannet AS1 was WN339 which made its initial flight from Northolt on June 9th 1953 piloted by Peter Twiss. From October 1954, Gannet AS1's were also assembled at Fairey's plant near Stockport, being test-flown from Ringway (now Manchester International Airport). The first Stockport AS1 was WN370, being demonstrated at Ringway on October 5th 1954 by David Masters, the unique network of footholds facilitating entry into the cockpit being the source of much consternation, later amusement, to all pilots making their first flight with the Gannet. A total of 172 Gannet AS1's were constructed as follows: –

WN339 – WN378
WN390 – WN429
WN445 – WN464
XA319 – XA364
XA387 – XA409
XA434 – XA436 and XD898 for Royal Australian Navy.

9

General in-flight views of VR557, the second Gannet prototype. Taken over Malta, operating from RNAS Hal Far.

Charles Brown

Charles Brown

A fine pair of aerial views of second prototype, VR557, overflying a submarine during exercises, with search equipment deployed and retracted. Also noticeable is the technique of feathering one propeller and throttling back one of its twin Mambas for increased endurance during search patrols.

11

Two slightly unusual aerial views of the Gannet AS1.

12

The third Gannet prototype, WE488. This aircraft is similar in appearance to all subsequent production aircraft.

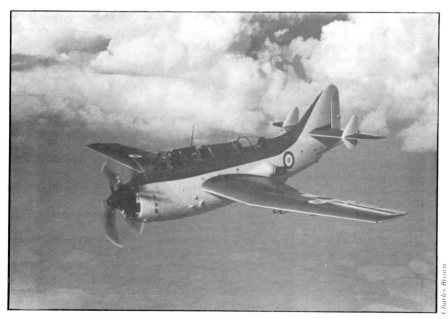

Aerial view of WE488, the third Gannet prototype utilised as the production prototype. WE488 was written-off in an accident at Turnhouse on 9 October 1953.

13

By the end of October 1953 the AS1 had completed its carrier trials and a Service Trials Unit, 703X Flight (703 Squadron) was formed at Ford Sussex. This undertook intensive flight trials, being commanded by Lt. Cdr. F.E. Cowton RN. The first operational Gannet AS1 Squadron, No 826 was formed at Lee-on-Solent on 17th January 1955 and embarked aboard H.M.S. Eagle in May of that year.

As the AS1 production proceeded at a pace, a trainer version, the Gannet T2 was being developed as a dual-control version of the AS1, the initial flight being undertaken on 16th August 1954 in WN365, a converted AS1. The T2 introduced dual controls into the second cockpit in place of the radar housing. Production of the Gannet T2 was integrated into the AS1 assembly lines at Hayes and Stockport and 36 were built as follows, WN365 Prototype: Converted from AS1, later converted to T5.

XA508 – XA530	(XA514 and XA517 delivered to the Royal Australian Navy).
XG869 – XG881	
XG888	Delivered to the Royal Australian Navy, returned to the Royal Navy and converted to a T5.
XG890	Delivered to the West German Navy as UA-99.

The Gannet MKS 1 and 2 were powered by the Double Mamba 100, and quickly recognised as being under-powered. Therefore Armstrong Siddeley developed an uprated Double Mamba 101 for the T4. The T2 was similar to the AS1 in appearance, except that the second cockpit had a retractable periscope visor for the instructor to see over the student's head. The Gannet T2 had folding wings, double-backed in characteristic Gannet style and the carrier landing gear was retained.

Gannet T2, XA510, taken in March 1955, believed to be just before delivery to the Royal Navy. The Gannet T2's were fitted with arrestor hooks as shown, but were rarely, if ever, used for deck landings aboard carriers at sea. Note the periscope over the student's cockpit to provide the instructor with adequate forward vision.

14

Delivery of the first Gannet AS1's to the Royal Navy, eventually to form the nucleus of 703X Squadron, the trials and development squadron, prior to entry to fully operational squadrons. The photograph is believed to have been taken at White Waltham in 1953.

Developments in anti-submarine warfare resulted in the next version of the Gannet, the AS4, incorporating the more powerful Double Mamba 101 A5MD3 engine to cater for the increased weight. Two homing torpedoes were now carried in the bomb bay along with parachute mines and depth charges, with provision for 16 rockets under the wings. The first flight took place on 13th April 1956, after which the AS4 followed on from the AS1 production lines at both Hayes and Stockport. Flight trials for the AS4 were conducted with WN372, a converted AS1. Ninety AS4's were built, supplementing Firefly AS6's, AS7's and Avengers and the Gannet AS4 completed the Fleet Air Arm's anti-submarine requirement. The AS4 was also scheduled to replace the Firefly in the R.N.V.R. (Air) anti-submarine squadrons at Ford, but all R.N.V.R. Air Squadrons were disbanded in March 1957 in the wake of the Suez Crisis. The serial numbers of the Gannet AS4's were:

XA412 – XA435
XA454 – XA474
XG788 – XG798
XG827 – XG855.

A few AS4's were refurbished in 1961, fitted with a new radar and electronics, and served with 831 Squadron at Culdrose. These included XA459, XA460, (ECM6); XA470 (COD6) and XA472. XA460 eventually became the only AS6 – ECM6 version to be used for trials by the new airborne-early warning squadron at Brawdy, Number 849, on the Gannet AEW3. Five AS4 airframes, XA430; XA454; XA466; XA470 and XG790 were converted into the Carrier-on-Board Delivery (COD4) with the anti-submarine search radar removed. The Gannet COD4 provided a robust, communication and special duties aircraft to link carriers at sea with shore bases and eventually one COD4 was allocated to each Gannet AEW3 Flight.

The dual-control version of the AS4 became the Gannet T5, which was very similar to the earlier T2. The last eight T2 production aircraft at Hayes, XG882 – XG889, were utilised for the T5 production batch, the first flight being made with

15

XG887 on March 1st 1957. Gannet T5's were mainly used by 849 Squadron at Culdrose and later Brawdy for initial and refresher pilot training.

Further views of the first Gannet AS1 deliveries to the Fleet Air Arm at White Waltham in the summer of 1953. Delays in the introduction of the Gannet had led to an interim delivery of 100 Grumman Avenger AS4's from the United States in 1951.

GANNET SQUADRONS

700 SQUADRON

Motto: Experienta docet (Experience teaches)

The Fleet Air Arm has always used the number in the '700' series as the development and trials squadron for new aircraft types being assessed for introduction into the Fleet. 700 Squadron re-formed at Ford on 18.8.55 with two Gannet AS1's, to be joined by Gannet T2's and AS4's from 1957-58.

700 Squadron became the Trials and Requirements Unit for the Gannet, being amalgamated from 703 and 771 Squadrons and moved to Yeovilton on 19.9.58 when RNAS Ford was closed as part of the Defence cuts of that year. The squadron disbanded on 3.7.61 with the remaining aircraft going to 771 Squadron.

Codings from 1956 were:
500 – 506 'FD' or 'VL'
520 – 522 'FD' or 'VL'
082 – 084 FD from aircraft amalgamated from 703 squadron.

Representative Aircraft were:
WN453/083; WN376/084.

703X FLIGHT

Motto: Experienta docet (Experience teaches)

The intensive flying trials unit for the Gannet AS1 formed at Ford on 15.3.54. Part of these trials involved cold weather operations in Canada and hot weather trials in Khartoum. The flight disbanded on 21.12.54 upon completion on the trials, the aircraft going to 700 Squadron.

Codes were 083 – 084 'FD'

Representative aircraft WN376 and WN453.

A line-up of 703X Squadron aircrew at RNAS FORD, Sussex, during development of the Gannet Service flying trials in 1953. 703X Squadron amassed an impressive total of flying hours to ensure the speedy introduction of the Gannet into front-line F.A.A. Anti-Submarine squadrons in early 1955.

Gannet AS1's of 703 X Squadron in formation operating from RNAS FORD.

19

719 SQUADRON

Motto: None

This squadron was often referred to as the Naval Air Anti-Submarine School, with 737 Squadron at RNAS Eglinton in Northern Ireland. Gannet AS1's arrived in November 1956, 719 absorbing 737 squadron on 22.11.57 to become the new Naval Anti-Submarine Operational School until disbanding on 17.3.59. The School operated a mixture of Gannet AS1's and T2's.

Codes were:
456 – 459 'GN' until 1956
541 – 559 'GN' from 1956

Representative aircraft were:

XA323/546/GN	XA352/551/GN
XA346/550/GN	XA357/545/GN
XA347/547/GN	XA522/542/GN

*A fine formation of Gannet AS1's from 719 Sqadron operating out of
RNAS EGLINTON.*

20

PILOT LANDS WITH BROKEN WINGS

With a third of each wing of his Fairey Gannet torn off Lieutenant Eric Taylor, a Fleet Air Arm pilot, continued to fly the aircraft and landed safely yesterday at Eglinton, Northern Ireland. Lieutenant Taylor was flying with another Gannet practising rocket firing on a range near Eglinton, and both aircraft were diving on a target at high speed. Pulling out of his dive Lieutenant Taylor's machine hit the slipstream of the other Gannet and the outer section of each wing broke away. Climbing to gain height before baling out, Lieutenant Taylor found he could still control the damaged aircraft, and determined to try to land. Experts who examined the aircraft believe that the luckiest thing was that both sections of the wing tore off at the same moment. If only one had been lost the plane would have gone out of control.

RNAS EGLINTON

21

728 SQUADRON

Motto: Descendo discimus (We learn
by teaching)

Relatively little has been placed on record concerning this second-line squadron, which
operated mainly as a Fleet Requirements Unit from Hal Far, Malta, using Gannet T2's
from July - November 1957.

737 SQUADRON

Motto: Purposeful

Reformed at Eglinton 30.3.49 as part of the 52nd Air Training Group. In 1950, 737 Squadron joined forces with 719 Squadron to form part of the Naval air Anti-Submarine School, both squadrons forming the 53rd Air Training Group. Gannet AS1's and T2's arrived in 1955, 737 Squadron disbanding and amalgamating into 719 Squadron on 22.11.57.

Codes used:
421 – 434 'GN' until 1956
617 – 627 'GN' from 1956

Gannets from 737 and 820 Squadrons from RNAS EGLINTON during a visit to the Fifth International Air Day at Ypenburg, Netherlands in May 1955.

23

Above:
Gannet AS.4, XA508/621 of 737 Squadron banking over Ulster on approach to RNAS Eglinton.
Right:
Lt. Cdr. D. Pennick, RN, CO of 737 Squadron, with two other unidentified aircrew posing in front of Gannet T2, XA508/421/ GN. Note the legend painted on the nose commemorating the squadron's appearance at the airshows at Ypenburg and Le Bourget.

744 SQUADRON:

Motto: Nemo solus satis sapit
(No one [or 'man'] knows enough)

Reformed on 1.3.54 at RNAS Culdrose Cornwall as part of the Naval Air-Sea War Development Unit, 744 Squadron moved to St. Mawgan on 23.10.54 to join forces with a similar Royal Air Force Unit. Initially using Firefly AS5's, Gannet AS1's arrived in November 1955. In October 1955, 744 Squadron was re-designated as the Naval Anti-Submarine Development Squadron and disbanded on 31.10.56.

Codes were:
401 – 403 'CU'

Representative aircraft were:
WN393; WN421; WN462; XA324.

796 SQUADRON

Motto: Ubi imus cognoscimus (We know
where we are going)

Reformed at St Merryn, Cornwall, on 13.11.47 as an Aircrewmans School, 796 Squadron changed its role and moved to Culdrose in February 1954. Along with 750 Squadron, 796 became the Observer and Air Signals School from early 1956, utilising Fireflies until Gannet AS1's and T2's arrived in February 1957. From March 1958 two Sea Balliols were used to convert Gannet pilots on to the new Skyraider.

Codes used:
761 – 784 'CU'

Representative aircraft:
XA324/762/CU

XA352/761/CU   XA398/780/CU
XA358/764/CU   XA399/773/CU
XA393/772/CU   XA404/776/CU
XA396/761/CU

810 SQUADRON

Motto: Ut fulmina de caelo (Like a
thunderbolt from heaven)

Originally an anti-submarine squadron between 1948–54, then a fighter squadron
active during the Suez crisis in 1956, 810 reformed at Culdrose on 20.4.59 as an
anti-submarine squadron again with six Gannet AS4's. Later in 1959, 810 embarked
in H.M.S. Centaur for a commission in the Mediterranean and the Far East,
returning via Australia in 1960, disbanding at Culdrose on 12.7.60.

Codes were:
230 – 236 'C'

Representative aircraft:
XA430/231/C
XA432/233/C
XA465/234/C
XA473/235/C

XA430/231 of 810 Squadron overflying CENTAUR during refuelling operations.

812 SQUADRON

Motto: Deis aie (God aid)

Famous as a Night-Fighter experimental squadron in 1948/49, followed by active service in Korea until 1953, 812 reformed at Eglinton on 7.11.55 as an anti-submarine squadron with 8 Gannet AS1's and a Gannet T2. The squadron embarked in H.M.S. Eagle in April 1956 for a Mediterranean work-up, during which the Suez crisis developed. 812's Gannets were replaced by 893 squadron's. Venoms in September 1956 to enhance Eagle's strike role. 812's Gannets flew ashore to Hal Far, Malta on 3 August 1956 and remained on standby there throughout the Suez affair in case of an anti-submarine threat before returning to Lee-on-Solent to disband on 13.12.56.

Codes used:
250 – 267 'J' or 'GN'

Representative aircraft:
XA339/256/J

814 SQUADRON

Motto: In hoc signo vinces (In this sign you will conquer)

One of the longest serving Fleet Air Arm post war squadrons, 814 has been involved in anti-submarine warfare since 1950. Reformed at Culdrose on 14.1.57 with 8 Gannet AS4's, embarking on board H.M.S Eagle on August Bank Holiday Monday, August 5th, along with 803 Squadron and 806 Squadron (Sea Hawks), 813 Squadron (Wyverns) and 894 Squadron (Sea Venoms). Eagle took part in Exercise 'Strike-back' in the North Atlantic and off the Norwegian coast before service in the Mediterranean. 814 spent time ashore at Hal Far, Malta before returning home to disband at Culdrose on 30.9.59. 814, in more recent times, achieved fame serving aboard H.M.S. Hermes in 1982 during the Falklands Conflict, with the Sea King HAS1.

Codes used:
280 – 288 'CU' or 'J' or 'E'

representative aircraft:
XA426/286/CU   XA454/281/E   XA456/283/E

Turning low over a very uninviting sea XA426/286 flying from EAGLE with 814 Squadron.

28

815 SQUADRON

Motto: Strike deep

Reformed at Eglinton on 6.2.56 as an anti-submarine Squadron with 8 Gannet AS1's plus a Gannet T2 for shore training. 815 embarked aboard Ark Royal in January 1957 for a visit to the U.S.A. and cross-operations with USS Saratoga in the Atlantic. Gannet AS4's replaced the AS1's in December 1957 and 815 disbanded at Culdrose on 15.7.58 after a Mediterranean cruise, again aboard Ark Royal. 815 in later years developed the use of helicopters in Fleet Air Arm Service from 1958 with the Wessex HAS-1.

Codes used:
290 – 299 'O' or 'R', with the Harp Badge on the finlets, due to the Squadrons' association with the maker of a well-known Irish beverage.

Representative aircraft:

XA321/293/0	XA337/296/0	XA340/292/0	XA344/294/0
XA336/291/0	XA338/290/0	XA341/295/0	XA354/298/0

At the point of no return from the port catapult on ARK ROYAL, XA340/292 of 815 Squadron. Note all the canopies are open for quick egress if the whole process ends up in the water.

29

820 SQUADRON

Motto: Tutamen et ultor (Safeguard and avenger)

Having been involved in anti-submarine operations since 1951 with Firefly AS5's, 820 Squadron was re-equipped with 9 Gannet AS1's at Eglinton on 7.3.55. The Squadron embarked aboard H.M.S. Centaur in January 1956 for a Mediterranean and Far East Commission, returning home on 15.5.56 for its AS1's to go into storage at Donibristle. 820 reformed at Eglinton on 30.7.56 with 8 Gannet AS1's, embarking aboard H.M.S. Bulwark in June 1957. The Squadron disbanded at Ford, Sussex, on 2.12.57. Currently. 820 Squadron operates the Sea King HAS5 as part of the Illustrious' Air Group.

Codes used:
401 – 409 'GN'
321 – 329 'C'
320 – 328 'C'

820's Gannets were identified by the purple and white stripes on the fins and finlets, nicknamed 'spangles'. The T2 trainers had yellow bands under the wing and around the fuselage.

Representative aircraft:
XA340/324/C
XA349/323/B
XA390/322/B
XA391/321/B
XA392/323/B
XA394/325/B
XA395/326/B
XA401/327/B
XA403/328/B

820 and 737 Squadron Gannets at Ypenburg, Netherlands, May 1955.

824 SQUADRON

Motto: Spectat ubique
spiritus (The wind everywhere
looks on)

An anti-submarine Squadron since 1952, 824 re-equipped with 8 Gannet AS1's in February 1955, initially aboard H.M.S. Bulwark before taking part in 'Exercise Dawn Breeze' from Ark Royal in October 55, during which, accused of carrying everything but a 'kitchen sink', an 824 Gannet dropped a kitchen-sink during a simulated anti-submarine strike. 824 disbanded at Ford on 17.4.56 to reform at Culdrose on 7.5.56, initially with 8 Gannet AS1's being replaced by 9 Gannet AS4's in October 56. The Squadron embarked onboard Ark Royal in January 1957. Transferring to H.M.S. Albion, disbanding at Culdrose on 1.11.57. In later years 824 Squadron became the first Sea King unit in 1970 aboard 'Ark Royal' and in 1982 operated the new Airborne Early Warning (AEW) Sea Kings before reformation of 849 Squadron.

Codes used: Representative aircraft:
411 – 419 'GN'   330 – 339 'Z' or 'A'   XA348/330/Z   XA363/333/Z
331 – 338 'O'   XA360/331/Z   XA362/332/Z

*The wire secure in the hook, a moment of relief and triumph for any naval Airman.
WN490/417 joins EAGLE from the shore base in Northern Ireland.*

32

825 SQUADRON

Motto: Nihil obstat (Nothing stops us)

Reformed at Culdrose on 4.7.55 an anti-submarine Squadron with 8 Gannet AS1's, embarking aboard H.M.S. Albion in January 1956 for a Far East Commission, returning to the United Kingdom to disband at Lee-on-Solent on 7.8.56. 825 reformed again at Culdrose on 6.5.57 with 9 Gannet AS4's flying to Hal Far, Malta in January 1958. The Squadron returned home to disband at Culdrose on 29.4.58.

Codes used:
340 – 348 'CU' or 'Z'

Representative aircraft:
XA319/346/Z   XA457/347/CU   XA461/345/CU
XA433/341/CU   XA458/348/CU   XA462/346/CU

825 Squadron Gannet A.S.4's 'beating-up' the airfield on one engine at Culdrose, July 4, 1955. Note the extended 'bins', which housed the radar.

33

826 SQUADRON

Motto: Latet anguis in aqua (A snake lies concealed in water)

The Gannet development programme having been delayed since 1954 826 re-equipped with 8 Gannet AS1's on 17.1.55 and embarked aboard H.M.S. Eagle in June for the NATO Exercise 'Sea Enterprise' off the Faeroes, returning to Lee-on-Solent and disbanding on 22.11.55, having proved the Gannet as an effective anti-submarine aircraft.

Codes:
271 – 279 'LS'
343 – 348 'J'

A series of fine operational photographs of 826 Squadron Gannets flying from EAGLE in the Mediterranean during the summer of 1955.

34

35

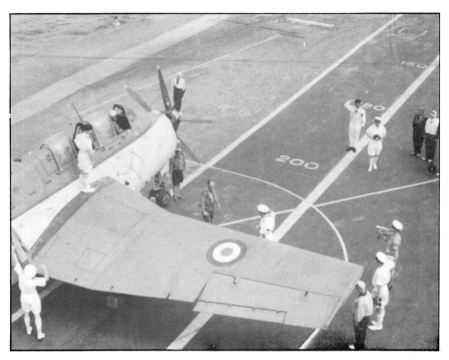

36

831 SQUADRON

Motto: Aquila non capit muscas (Eagles
don't catch flies)

Reformed at Culdrose 1.5.58 as an Electronics Warfare Squadron by renumbering 751 Squadron. 'A' Flight used two Gannet AS1's as well as Gannet ECM4's and ECM6's. In 1960 831 won the Boyd Trophy for outstanding services to Fleet Training. 831 moved to RAF Watton in Norfolk for joint RAF work, disbanding there on 26.8.66 by merging into 360 Squadron RAF.

Codes used:
265 – 280, normally minus the 'CU' tail code.

Representative aircraft:
XA340/279
XA472/278

847 SQUADRON

Motto: Ex alto concutimus (We shake
them from on high)

Reformed on 17.3.56 from part of 812 Squadron at Eglinton for service in Cyprus with 3 Gannet AS1's, 847 was based at Nicosia for daily patrols to detect arms smuggling, the AS1's being replaced by three AS4's in June 1958.

The Squadron disbanded upon returning to Yeovilton on 1.12.59. In May 1982 the Squadron was hurriedly reformed as a Commando Squadron with Wessex helicopters. The Squadron served with distinction in the Falklands Conflict and after this brief moment of glory was disbanded in September 1982.

Codes used:
086 – 088 (The AS1's had a 'HF' tail code)

Representative aircraft:
XA335/086/HF

CHANNEL AIR DIVISION –
1840 + 1842 RNVR SQUADRONS

Motto: Allied and avenging

1840 Squadron reformed at Culham on 14.4.51 as a Royal Naval Volunteer Reserve Anti-Submarine Squadron, later moving to Ford to form the Channel Air Division of the RNVR, principally from ex-FAA 'regular' aircrew who wished to maintain a part-time link with the service. 1840 received 11 Gannet AS1's and T2's from February 1956, and formed a very enthusiastic and effective role, principally flying at weekends with the bonus of an annual cruise. Sadly, following the Defence Review in the wake of Suez, all RNVR Squadrons were disbanded on 10.3.57. 1842 Squadron was pooled with 1840 Squadron and both Squadrons shared the Gannets.

Codes used:
875 – 884 'FD'

Representative aircraft:
XA387/877/FD
XA398/878/FD

EXPORT GANNETS

The success of the Gannet in the anti-submarine role naturally attracted attention from overseas and although the Gannet never achieved the export status of the Hunter, nevertheless respectable orders were received from Australia, West Germany and Indonesia. Further interest came from India, Canada and the Netherlands but no firm orders were received, probably due to American competition. Australia had commissioned the light carrier H.M.S. Terrible as H.M.A.S. Sydney in 1948, later to serve with distinction in the Korean War. In 1952 the light carrier H.M.S. Vengence was loaned to the Australians on account of the delay in completing the former H.M.S. Majestic upon which all work had ceased in 1945. Majestic became commissioned as the new H.M.A.S. Melbourne in November 1955, resplendent with her new angled flight deck and latest carrier technology. Melbourne undertook her sea trials and work up in U.K. waters, the Gannets operating initially from RNAS Culdrose, before arriving in Australia in April 1956 with their complement of Sea Venom FAW 53's of 808 Squadron and Gannets from 816 and 817 Squadron. The Royal Australian Navy ordered 33 AS1's and 3 Gannet T2's which retained their British serials as follows:

Gannet AS1: WN456 – 459

XA350;	XA351	XA326;	XA334
XA389;	XA403	XA356;	XA359
XD898;	XA784	XA434;	XA436
XG789;	XG791	XG785;	XG787
XG796;	XG825	XG792;	XG795
XG826;			

Gannet T2:
XA514; XA517
XA531 – later cancelled and replaced by XD898.

AUSTRALIAN GANNET SQUADRONS

724 SQUADRON

Motto: Learn and live

A second line unit operating mainly as an Operational Training School 724 had reformed at RNAS Nowra on 1.6.55 with Fireflies, Sea Vampires and later Gannets. In January 1958, 724 Squadrons' Gannets were transferred to 725 Squadron.

Codes and Representative aircraft:
XA326/880/NW
XA329/973/NW
XA330/882/NW
XA350/881/NW
XA514/878/NW
XA517/876/NW

725 SQUADRON

Motto: Be aggressive

Reformed at RNAS Nowra on 13.1.58 as a General Fleet Requirements Unit for the Royal Australian Navy with Fireflies, Sea Venoms and 2 Gannets AS1's and a T2. In May 1959 the Squadron changed into an anti-submarine training unit, but disbanded on 31.5.61 by being absorbed into 724 Squadron.

816 SQUADRON

Motto: Imitate the action of the tiger

Since 1948, 816 Squadron has been a Royal Australian Navy unit and served with distinction in Korea. 816 reformed and worked up at Culdrose with 7 Gannet AS1's from August 1955 until departure for Australia in early 1956, aboard H.M.A.S. Melbourne. Disbanded at RNAS Nowra in August 15th 1967.

Codes used:
300 – 306 'M' or 'Y' with a Kangaroo on the tail emblem

Representative aircraft:
XA327/305/Y
XA328/304/Y
XA330/302/Y
XA331/301/Y
XA332/300/Y

A fine photograph of 816 and 817 Squadrons of the Royal Australian Navy, equipped with the Gannet AS1 816 used codes 421-426/B with codes 431-435 being allocated to 817 Squadron. The location.is Royal Naval Air Station Culdrose (HMS Seahawk) in 1955/56 just prior to the Squadron's embarkation aboard the new carrier HMAS MELBOURNE for the voyage to Australia. Note the standard Fleet Air Arm Control Tower with the original small visual control centre on top, replaced by the vastly more modern device in the early 1960's.

Charles Brown Photo

43

817 SQUADRON

Motto: Aude facere (Dare to act)

Reformed at Culdrose on 18.8.55 with 7 Gannet AS1's serving aboard Sydney and Melbourne between 1955 and 1958, shore-based at RNAS Nowra, where it disbanded on 18.8.58.

Codes used: *Representative aircraft:*
310 – 316 'Y'   XA334/313/Y   XA350/316/Y

In December 1959, the Australian Government announced that Carrier operations would cease in 1963 when the Venoms and Gannets would be retired and the carriers scrapped. However in 1960 H.M.A.S. Melbourne gained a reprieve as an anti-submarine carrier with an enhanced role for the Gannet. The growing unrest in the Far East in the early 1960's, especially from Indonesia and communist China, led to a reappraisal of the Australian Naval Air Arm and in 1967 the Venoms and Gannets were replaced by A4D-5 Skyhawks and S2F-3 Trackers respectively. In more recent times, the Australian Government gave up its fixed-wing carrier capability but in view of recent world events many Australians regard the premature demise of their naval aviation capability, as is the United Kingdom, as a cause for concern.

GANNETS WITH THE WEST GERMAN NAVY

The mid 1950's witnessed the initial re-arming of West Germany, now firmly a member of the North Atlantic Alliance, the Gannet being ordered for the new German Naval Air Arm, the Kriegsmarine. Conversion onto the Gannet was managed by Fairey's themselves at their experimental base at White Waltham under the direction of Roy Morris, two courses of six pilots were put through 50 hours flying training using two T5's and four Gannets AS4's. The pilots then transferred to Eglinton from May 1958 to work up with their new crews. West Germany ordered 15 AS4's and one T5, diverted from a cancelled Royal Navy batch as follows

AS4's:

XG829/UA114	XG834/UA102	XG839/UA105	XG844/UA108
XG830/UA115	XG835/UA103	XG840/UA106	XG846/UA109
XG833/UA101	XG836/UA104	XG843/UA107	XG849/UA110

44

XG850/UA111   *T5's*
XG852/UA112   XG890/UA99
XG853/UA113

All German Gannets were in sea-grey with white undersides and Marineflieger anchor insignia. Following completion of their training at Eglinton, German Gannets were flown to Schleswig, on the Baltic Coast, for anti-submarine duties with MFG-3 (Graf Zeppelin) Squadron, which had formed at Eglinton in 1958. MFG-3 moved to Nordholz in 1965 to re-equip with the Breguet Atlantic and all the Kriegsmarine Gannets were withdrawn in 1967–68.

A fine photograph of the Kriegsmarine's (West German Navy) one Gannet T5, UA-99, used to train German Gannet air-crew at Schleswig on the Baltic Coast. West Germany received 15 Gannet AS4's and one T5 from 1958. All Kreigsmarine Gannets were painted sea-grey with white undersides and Marineflieger anchor insignia.

GANNETS WITH THE INDONESIAN NAVY

The final export order of the Gannet came in January 1959 when the Indonesian Naval Air Arm ordered 18 aircraft. To meet this order Fairey's bought 20 AS1's and 2 T2's from the Ministry of Supply for modification of equipment to AS4's and T5's, with airframe sections for two new AS4'S and one T5. Fairey's again established a training programme at White Waltham in 1959/60 with 14 aircraft, including the T2 prototype, WN365, which had been brought up to T5 standard, WN365 then became registered by Fairey as G-AYPO and later re-registered for the Royal Navy as XT572.

Serials for the Indonesian Gannets were:

AS-00 to AS-17

Views of the Gannet AS4's and T5's on trials before delivery to the Indonesian Naval Arm, taken in the summer of 1959, probably at Fairey's White Waltham airfield. Indonesia ordered 20 Gannet AS1's and two T2's for modification by the Ministry of Supply to AS4 and T5 standard.

AIRBORNE EARLY WARNING - THE GANNET AEW3

The requirement for airborne early warning at sea had its origins in the Pacific Campaigns during World War II, when the 'Kamikaze' suicide pilots attempted to disrupt the Allied Carrier Task Forces. The immediate post-war situation left the Royal Navy with world wide responsibilities at a time when both aircraft and missile technology was developing at an alarming rate. To ensure its survival against this increased threat, the Fleet Air Arm immediately looked into the provision of radar early warning at sea.

The main problem confronting shipborne radar is that transmissions can only travel along a relatively straight line and are unable to follow the earth's curvature. Thus, it is relatively easy for ships and aircraft to approach a Task Force and only be detected in the latter stages of their attack, often giving only a couple of minutes advance warning to the defenders. The only way to counteract this threat is to take the radar into the air, hence the evolution of the concept of airborne early warning (AEW). In particular the advent of the new generation of fast jet aircraft posed a serious threat to surface warships.

The U.S. Navy initiated the 'Cadillac' programme in 1945, using a Grumman Avenger and a basic radar system, meeting with only partial success. Several Douglas Skyraider aircraft were similarly modified and the Royal Navy were sufficiently encouraged to order 50 Skyraider AEW's under the Mutual Defence Aid Programme to equip 849 Squadron from 1952. By the mid 1950's the limitations of the Skyraider were such that the Admiralty began to search for more suitable equipment and aircraft. The robust airframe of the Gannet AS1 provided the obvious choice and Fairey were directed to design a revised version of the Gannet airframe to house the radar, and an uprated version of the successful Double Mamba engine.

The Gannet AEW3 had a crew of pilot, observer and radar operator, housing an AN/APS-20E search radar , giving the characteristic 'bulge' under the fuselage.

Power was supplied by the Bristol Siddely Double Mamba Mk 112 (DM8) gas turbine engine, giving the same advantages of twin-engined aircraft as experienced in the anti-submarine Gannet. The Double Mamba gave an endurance of approximately five hours and the power-folding assisted stowage aboard the limited hangers of Royal Navy Carriers. The Gannet AEW3 developed into a very effective airborne early warning system and information from the aircraft would quickly be processed via the radar relay link ART-28 known as 'Bellhop' to the parent carrier, a process which in this age of computer jargon would be called a data-link. A prototype and 44 production Gannet AEW's were ordered, whilst a converted AS1, WN345, had been used since 1956 to develop the Double Mamba 112 ASMD8 engine.

XJ440:

The prototype Gannet AEW3 made its first flight from Northolt with Peter Twiss on 20.8.58, later being used for trials at White Waltham. XJ440 was painted in full RN markings and took part in the 1958 Farnborough Air Display, before landing onboard H.M.S. Centaur for carrier trials on 18.11.58. Further trials were undertaken at Boscombe Down before the aircraft was transferred to Filton for engine trials, where it sadly was destroyed in a flying accident on 26.4.60.

Production serials for the Gannet AEW3 were: –

XJ440   XP197 – XP199   XL449 – XL456   XP224 – XP229
XL471 – XL482   XR431 – XR433   XL493 – XL503

The first production aircraft, XL449, first flew on 2.12.58 and was used to test the radar and operational equipment before joining 849 Squadron in 1962. XL450 was used initially for deck landing trials aboard H.M.S. Victorious before undertaking hot weather trials in Libya in July 1959.

Fairey Aviation Co Ltd

The prototype Gannet AEW3, XJ440 during trials in the summer of 1958. No radar equipment was ever installed in this aircraft, which was utilised purely to develop the flying capabilities of the AEW3.

Front view of XJ440, the AEW 3 prototype.

Gannet AEW 3 prototype XJ440.

49

A ground shot of XJ440 during trials in the summer of 1958.

Peter Twiss in XJ440 - note footholds in the panels beneath the cockpit.

50

Lucas Aviation Co. Ltd.

A fine view of XJ440, the Gannet AEW3 prototype, on trials before entry in service, during the summer of 1958. The Airfield on the right is believed to be Northolt - one can hardly imagine test-flying on prototypes being undertaken in such close proximity to London Airport today!

Yeovil RAeS / F. Ballam

Above and following pages, a wonderful series of photographs showing prototype Gannet AEW XJ440 on trials, now in its Royal Navy Colours.

51

Yeovil RAeS / F. Ballam

Yeovil RAeS / F. Ballam

Yeovil RAeS / F. Ballam

Yeovil RAeS / F. Ballam

Yeovil RAeS / F. Ballam

Yeovil RAeS / F. Ballam

Yeovil RAeS / F. Ballam

Heave! Flight-deck party ranging XL451 aboard VICTORIOUS. Note inner set of props rotating to assist in manoeuvring, and the pair of Sea Venoms in the background.

*A fine shot of XL451 about to undertake a non-assisted launch from VICTORIOUS.
Note the Scimitar and Sea Venom parked to the rear of the radar mast.*

*A fine aerial shot of the flight-deck of VICTORIOUS with XL451 being readied for launch.
Note the other fixed-wing aircraft of the period, in the form of the Sea Venom, Sea Vixen,
Scimitar and the forerunner of the Gannet AEW3 - the Skyraider!*

56

XL451 about to be launched from VICTORIOUS. Note the mirror landing system and the Dragonfly plane-guard to the right.

XL451 at the point of launch from VICTORIOUS. Note the Sea Vixen being ranged on deck and the centre deck well for the lift – a characteristic feature of Royal Navy carriers, as opposed to the U.S. Navy who favoured the side lift.

Geronimo!'... XL451 leaving the flight deck with the Dragonfly helicopter guard to the right, ready to winch-up aircrew in the event of a duching.

GANNET AEW3 UNITS

700 SQUADRON 'G' FLIGHT

This became the AEW Intensive Trials Unit which formed at Culdrose on 17.8.59 under the command of Lt Cdr. W. Hawley R. N., using Gannet AEW3's XL453-5. By January 1960 the flight had amassed over 1,000 hours, an incredible feat for such a small flight. 700 'G' Flight was absorbed by 849 Squadron 'A' Flight at Culdrose on 1.2.60.

849 SQUADRON

Motto: Primus video (The first to see)

849 Squadron became the sole front-line operator of the Gannet AEW3 with a headquarters Flight permanently shore-based and Flights detached for service on board the carriers. The normal complement of a Flight was 4 Gannet AEW3's plus a 'COD' – an AS4 for Carrier on Board Delivery which consisted of communication and general duties. The Flights were parented ashore with the H.Q. Flight when the carrier was in refit. All 849 Squadron Gannet AEW3's had sky-coloured fuselages with extra dark sea grey on the upper surfaces. All letter and code numbers were in black. 849 Squadron can rightfully claim to be Airborne Early Warning as far as the Royal Navy is concerned. Apart from a six year break (1978-1984), it has been the Royal Navy's front line AEW Squadron since 1952 when it operated the Skyraider and is currently operating the Sea King AEW Mk 2 helicopter.

849 H.Q. FLIGHT:

This unit was responsible for training and backup for the carrier borne Flights, based initially at Culdrose (CU). The Squadron moved to RNAS Brawdy in December 1964 and finally to Lossiemouth in November 1970 where it disbanded along with 'B' Flight on 15.12.78 after the de-commissioning of Ark Royal.

Codes:
410 – 416 'CU' 'BY' or 'LM'
760 – 768 'LM'

Representative aircraft:
XL473/410/CU
XL497/411/CU

Gannet AEW3 XL456/413/CU of 849 Squadron HQ Flight at Culdrose in the early 1960's. 849 Squadron moved to Brawdy in December 1964, ending its long career with the Gannet AEW3 at Lossiemouth in 1978.

Gannet AEW3 XL502/764/BY of 849 HQ Flight at Brawdy in the late 1960's.

The characteristic wing fold of the Gannet in progress as XL453 taxies in.

849 SQUADRON 'A' FLIGHT:

Formed at Culdrose on 1.2.60 under Lt Cdr W. Hawley RN, previous C.O. of 700 G Squadron, replacing the Douglas Skyraider aboard Ark Royal in March 1960. In the early 1960's 'A' Flight sported red and black spinner markings and on the rear of the finlets. For a time 'A' Flight displayed the letter 'A' and a red Albatross on the fin. 'A' Flight saw extensive service aboard the Royal Navy's carriers as follows:

Ark Royal
(R)   Embarked onboard for a Mediterranean Cruise on 3.3.60.

Centaur
(C)   Embarked for a Far East Commission from April 1961 until Spring 1963.

Victorious
(V)   Embarked from August 1963 for further service in the Far East, disbanded 27.7.65 at Brawdy. Reformed 20.1.66 at Brawdy for service aboard Victorious until Spring 1967.

Hermes
(H)   Embarked on 29.5.68 for a Far East Commission, disbanded at Brawdy on 14.7.70 after Hermes last commission as a fixed-wing conventional carrier.

Codes:
420 – 423 until 1965
260 – 264 until 1970.

Representative aircraft:
XL472/421/R   XL502/260/H
XL473/422/R   XL479/261/V
XL474/423/R

A Gannet AEW3 of 849 Squadron 'A' Flight aboard VICTORIOUS in the early 1960's. 'A' Flight used codes in the 420-423 range and the 'V' for VICTORIOUS between 1960-1965.

62

Gannet AEW3 XL454/261/H of 849 Squadron 'A' Flight, normally operated from HERMES. Photo taken during a detachment to Brawdy in the late 1960's.

'Hands to Flying Stations!' Ground crew prepare Gannet AEW3, XL503/263/V, on left and a Gannet COD4 on the right for the day's flying programme. Note how the double-folded wings enable the aircraft to be ranged close together on deck, and the dark colouring of the COD4.

63

Yeovil RAeS/ F. Ballam

A Gannet AEW3 of 849 Squadron 'A' Flight, XL503/263/V, is ranged and lined up along the line of the steam catapult aboard VICTORIOUS. Flight deck personnel must surely have experienced one of the most potentially dangerous occupations imaginable! Note the Sea Vixen parked in the right background.

Yeovil RAeS/ F. Ballam

Gannet AEW3, XR432/262/V of 849 Squadron 'A' Flight launches from VICTORIOUS. Occasionally, Gannets were able to launch without the assistance of steam-catapults - an experience not for the faint-hearted!

Yeovil RAeS/F. Ballam

A fine shot of an 849 Squadron 'A' Flight Gannet AEW3, XL481/260/V, about to recover aboard VICTORIOUS. Taken on a fine day with a calm sea, there were many occasions when conditions were much more difficult to recover fixed-wing aircraft aboard HM carriers.

Yeovil RAeS/F. Ballam

Gannet AEW3 XR432/232/V on final approach to VICTORIOUS. Note the arrester hook deployed.

65

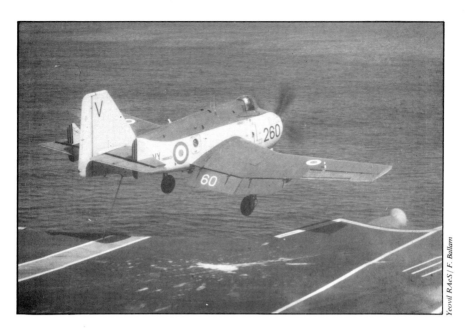

Yeovil RAeS / F. Ballam

Gannet AEW3, XL481/260/V of 849 Squadron 'A' Flight after apparently aborting a landing aboard VICTORIOUS. Note the fully extended arrestor hook.

J. Maclachlan

Gannet COD4, XA454, Flag Officer Aircraft Carrier's 'barge', being launched from VICTORIOUS.

66

849 SQUADRON 'B' FLIGHT:

'B' Flight was the longest serving Flight of Gannet AEW3's, surviving until the demise of Ark Royal at the end of 1978. In addition, 'B' Flight served aboard most of the RN's carrier force as follows:

Victorious	(V)	Served abroad during 1961/62 in the Mediterranean and Far East.
Centaur	(C)	Embarked from 22.12.63 until 11.5.65, disbanded 12.9.65 at Brawdy after Centaur's last commission.
Hermes	(H)	Embarked from 16.5.62 to 27.9.63 in the Far East, before transferring to Centaur. Reformed 18.4.66 for further service aboard Hermes, disbanded at Brawdy 28.2.68.
Ark Royal	(R)	Reformed 5.1.70 at Brawdy for Ark Royal's modernised role with 809 Squadron Buccaneers and 892 Squadron Phantoms, saw continuous service until late 1978. On 27 November 1978, four 'B' Flight Gannet AEW3's launched from Ark Royal for the last time and transited via Yeovilton to Lossiemouth, where the Flight disbanded on 15.12.78. An 849 'B' Gannet had the honour of making the last fixed wing recovery aboard Ark Royal earlier in that week.

Codes:
425 – 428 (pre 1965)
330 – 333 (1965–68)
040 – 044 (1970–78)

Representative aircraft:
XP225/425/C
XP227/427/C
XL497/041/R
XL450/042/R
XL471/042/R
XL472/044/R

In the early 1960's 'B' Flight Gannets had black and yellow bands on the spinners, a 'bee' on the fin and the arrestor hook also in black and yellow banding. The roundel was in the standard red, white and blue. By the 1970's, the roundel was altered to NATO low-visibility red and blue and fin markings of black and yellow triangles with the 'busy bee'.

Gannet AEW3 XP227/427/H of 849 Squadron 'B' Flight takes the wire on landing aboard HERMES. Fixed wing operations demanded a steady nerve, robust undercarriage and, occasionally, more than an element of luck!

Gannet AEW3 XL454/331/H of 849 Squadron 'B' Flight, whose parent carrier was HERMES. Taken in the late 1960's.

68

Gannet AEW3 XL471/070/E of 849 Squadron 'B' Flight from EAGLE, taken at Hal Far, Malta in the early 1970's. Note the 'Red Dragon' fin symbol, taken from the Chinese game of Mah-Jongg.

Gannet AEW3, XP225/072/E of 849 'D' Flight, believed taken at Brawdy in the early 1970's when detached from the parent carrier, EAGLE.

849 'C' FLIGHT

'C' Flight was formed to serve aboard H.M.S. Hermes and embarked on 5 July 1960, transferring to Ark Royal from 13.11.61. The Flight achieved fame for its work off Mozambique during the Beira Patrol for which it won the Boyd Trophy in 1966. 'C' Flight disbanded at Brawdy after Ark Royal's return to the United Kingdom on 5.10.66. 'C' Flight Gannets displayed black and white spinners, with black and white stripes on the finlets and arrestor hooks.

Codes:
430 – 433

Fly-past by four Gannet AEW3's from 849 Squadron in the early 1960's, XL494/432/H, XL501/433/H, XL471/430/H, believed to be from 'C' Flight aboard HERMES, and XL454/410 from HQ Flight at Culdrose.

849 'D' FLIGHT

'D' Flight formed for service aboard H.M.S. Eagle (E) embarking on 2 December 1964 for service in the Far East. The Flight stayed with Eagle until she returned after her final commission in late 1971, disbanding at Lossiemouth on 26.11.72. 'D' Flight Gannets also used black and white spinners and at some time sported a Red Dragon emblem on the fin.

Codes:
435 – 438 (pre 1965)
070 – 074 (1965–72)

Representative aircraft:
XP225/072/E

1966 AND ALL THAT....

Readers may well remember the satirical book and play '1066 And All That' from their school history lessons. The Fleet Air Arm can be forgiven for regarding the 1966 Defence White Paper with equal derision, for up to that infamous document, naval aviation was poised for a bright future stretching until the turn of the century. The decade of the 1950's had witnessed a dramatic increase in the capability of the Fleet Air Arm, highlighted with new angled flight decks, mirror landing sights and a new generation of jet aircraft that were equal to any potential adversary. The Gannet AEW3 was a product of this new initiative in naval aviation and formed an indispensible element of the Royal Navy's Carrier Task Forces that were responsible for peace-keeping in many parts of the world, especially in the Far East. From Korea to Malaya and Kuwait, the flexibility of an integrated carrier task force had been demonstrated to good effect. The Cuban Crisis in late 1962, in which the Soviet Union had backed down in the face of superior U.S. Navy forces, backed by nuclear force, provided ample demonstration of the necessity to maintain a strong maritime capability. In Britain, studies were in an advanced stage to provide the Fleet Air Arm with new carriers and aircraft for the foreseeable future, with the Gannet replacement being a high priority. The pinnacle of the new Fleet Air Arm was to be the new carrier, CVA01. Blackburn, the famous aircraft producers of Royal Navy aircraft over several decades, produced the outstanding Buccaneer low level strike aircraft in 1958, with its ability to fly well below shipborne radar defence systems. The very success of the Buccaneer in turn caused alarm at the Admiralty, on the supposition that the Warsaw Pack might copy the same technology. In the United States, Grumman had developed the outstanding E-2 Hawkeye, but the price was out of the range of the United Kingdom. The Gannet AEW3 replacement was given an immediate increase in priority and in January 1963 the Admiralty issued Naval Air Specification 6166 for aircraft designers to to produce proposals for the airbourne early warning system for the new generation of carriers.

The design team at Brough initially favoured an AEW version of their outstanding Buccaneer, with two sideways-facing radar antennae inserted in the rotating bomb-bay. This very cost-effective solution would have enabled a Buccaneer AEW to cruise at up to 40,000 feet, giving a range of over 250 miles for the radar systems. By late 1963 Brough had developed the idea of proposing a Buccaneer airframe with a Blue Parrot radar in the nose and a new radar in the tail — in effect the 'fore and aft' radar scanner principle developed in the later Nimrod AEW. The possible solution of a large radome mounted above the aircraft, as utilised in the Grumman E-2, was looked on with disfavour by the Admiralty, for problems of stowage aboard its carriers.

A later consideration involved a similar fitting to the new H.S.125 jet, but eventually the Brough team came out in favour of their P.139 design, similar in shape to the Lockheed S-3A Viking but with provision for the 'fore and aft' radar scanners. The P.139 was to be powered by two Rolls Royce RB172/T – 260B engines which were later destined to power the new Anglo-French Jaguar. The Admiralty were to delay the implementation of the P.139 by their insistence of fitting a quart in a pint pot whereby the P.139 was to have Carrier-On-Board

Delivery (COD) capability. In view of the impending change in the political scene in Britain, this delay was to prove costly indeed. For the moment, however, the Fleet Air Arm was looking forward to a promising future and assembled itself at Yeovilton in May of 1964 to celebrate its Golden Jubilee.

Life however, is never predictable and, with a change of Government in October of 1964, ominous clouds were gathering over the horizon for fixed-wing naval aviation. For reasons which are still beyond comprehension, Wilson's new government targetted the British Aircraft Industry as the focus for their disfavour and cancelled many outstanding projects, such as the TSR2 strike attack aircraft and a whole range of promising new designs. How the Americans and French must have rejoiced! During 1965 a change in attitude towards the Royal Navy became apparent, culminating in the infamous 1966 Defence Review, which cancelled CVA-01 and aimed to eliminate the existing carrier force upon withdrawal from East of Suez by the early 1970's. Mr Healey, the then Defence Minister, poured scorn on the suggestion that the carrier force should be retained and sadly, allowed his own personal prejudice against fixed-wing naval aviation to cloud his judgement over future decisions on the re-equipment of the Royal Navy.

The First Sea Lord Sir David Luce and Christopher Mayhew, the Navy Minister, resigned but such was the atmosphere in the M.O.D. at the time, when the RAF was vigorously proposing a series of world-wide land bases, that the anti-carrier lobby carried the day. The events of this unhappy period are well chronicled in Dennis Wettern's book 'The Decline of British Sea Power since 1945' and insofar as this book is concerned, a key point in the 1966 review was the deletion of any reference to the future provision of any form of airborne early warning for the Fleet. Writing in the September 1966 of 'Navy', Captain G.C. Baldwin R.N. (Ret'd) disclosed that, when he had been Director of Naval Warfare, Mr Healey had cancelled plans for replacement of the AEW Gannet. 'It was not only the Navy that suffered here, the new aircraft was just as eagerly sought after by the R.A.F. to give the Army warning of low level strike aircraft over land. (Gannets had performed this role during the Indonesian Confrontation in 1964). The cancellation of the Gannet AEW replacement may one day be recognised as a greater national loss than either the TSR2 or the F.111'. Sixteen years later, after continual 'fudging' by successive Defence Ministers, Capt Baldwins prediction was to be tragically fulfilled in the South Atlantic.

Hardly had the ink dried on the 1966 Review when events in Rhodesia forced Mr Healey to demonstrate the effective peace-time role of the Royal Navy's carrier force as never before. In order to effect sanctions upon the illegal Smith regime. Wilson's Government tried to establish a blockade of the Port of Beira in Mozambique in an effort to force the white minority Government to the negotiating table. For many months, Gannet AEW3's from Eagle and later Ark Royal, assisted by Sea Vixens and Buccaneers, undertook the extensive task of identifying shipping in the Mozambique Channel and 'escorted' oil tankers away from the area. The Beira Patrol was one of the most successful if exhausting post-war Royal Navy operations which never received its full justification in the press at home from a Government which if it noticed the Fleet Air Arm's role at all, cared even less.

By the late 1960's, the carrier strength of the Royal Navy was depleted even further with the elimination of H.M.S. Victorious from the active list following a minor dockyard fire at Portsmouth. Hermes returned from a Far East Commission in 1970 to face conversion into a commando carrier, by which time 849 Squadron was reduced to just a Headquarters Unit and Flights aboard Eagle and Ark Royal. The light carrier H.M.S. Centaur was reduced to the role of an accommodation ship for crews of carriers in refit and the run-down of the Fleet Air Arm's remaining fixed wing Squadrons of Sea Vixens and Buccaneers began in earnest.

Westland Aircraft

The beginning of the end. Gannet AEW3 XL494 being rolled-out at Westland's Weston factory in late 1975, the last AEW3 to be refurbished and, sadly, ending a 60-year long association between Westland and fixed-wing naval aviation. Note the two explosive system warning triangles under the cockpit, one for the canopy and one for underwater ejection, and also the latest two-colour NATO-type roundels.

Hopes of a reprieve for fixed-wing naval aviation was revived with the election of the Heath Government in June 1970, but apart from the completion of Ark Royal's massive 3-year refit the pattern of fixed-wing elimination was continued. Eagle was present at the farewell fly-past to the British presence at Singapore in October 1971 following which she was used for spare parts to keep her sister, Ark Royal in service until the late 1970's. This left 849 Squadrons Gannet AEW3's reduced to the role of a Headquarters at 'B' Flight at Lossiemouth. Extensive overhauls to prolong the lives of the remaining Gannets took place at Westland's Ilchester plant, whilst the Lossiemouth spare Gannets were kept in storage and rotated to preserve their active life. The last Gannet to be refurbished by Westland was XL494 which, when handed back to the Royal Navy on 12th February 1976 ended a 60 year association between Westland and fixed-wing naval aviation. The Gannet AEW3 as built was also the

73

Final operations of the Gannet AEW3 took place from the RN's last conventional carrier, ARK ROYAL, from 1970-1978. 849 Squadron 'B' Flight adopted the 'Busy Bee' fin emblem, together with codes 040-044. Here Gannet AEW3 XL471/043/R shows the final markings, including the standard NATO roundel, whilst shore-based at Lossiemouth in the mid 1970's.

The End of the Road. After ARK ROYAL's decommissioning at the end of 1978, 849's Gannets (HQ and 'B' Flight) were mainly cut up on site at Lossiemouth, their shells being dumped aroung the airfield perimeter. Here, the remains of XL479/044/R lie outside 849 Squadron's hangar at Lossiemouth.

last of many Fairey aircraft to serve with the Royal Navy. Work on another AEW3 XL480, was stopped due to the defence cuts of that year.

Ark Royals' last commission, with 849 Squadron 'B' Flight Gannets embarked, took place in 1978. Monday 27th November 1978 witnessed the last conventional carrier launches from a British warship when Ark Royals' Buccaneers (809 Squadron), Phantoms (892 Squadron) and Gannets (XL497/R/041; XL450/R/042; XL471/R/043; XL472/R/044) were launched from Ark Royal off Gibraltar to return to the U.K. Ark's last return to Devonport closed the long chapter of Royal Navy conventional carrier operations, the Buccaneers and Phantoms being transferred to the RAF and the Gannets relegated to the fire dump at Lossiemouth, 849 Squadron officially disbanded on 15th December 1978. The anti-carrier lobby initiated by Mr Healey in 1965 had finally won and although fixed-wing naval aviation made a revival in 1980 with the introduction of the Sea Harrier from the new 'Through Deck Cruisers', no provision at all was made for airborne early warning in the Fleet. Within four years, the folly of this situation was vividly displayed to the world in the Falklands Conflict where, with supreme irony, the lack of AEW, which the Royal Navy had helped to pioneer three decades earlier, was to result in grievous losses.

A unique photograph of AEW3 XR433 showing early experiments in the Decca E.S.M., flying from Yeovilton in 1967.

SUPERIOR ACCOMMODATION FOR TWO

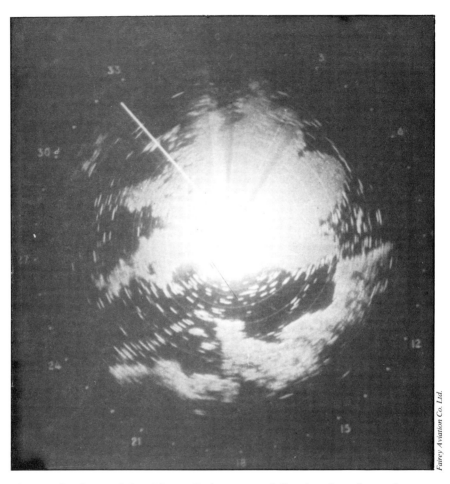

Fatey Aviation Co. Ltd.

Photograph of one of the airborne Radar screens, believed to have been taken over Oxfordshire, at a height of 18000', giving a range of 200 nautical miles. Operators certainly had to be able to distinguish targets from 'clutter'.

An interesting photograph taken inside the Gannet's fuselage showing the radar console. In this modern age of electronic wizardry, the Gannet's radar looks rather archaic. It is, perhaps, a sobering thought that at the time of writing, these radar sets, having been transferred from the Gannet to the Royal Air Force in the late 1970's, still form the mainstay of Britain's airborne early warning system with 8 Squadron's Shackletons! The politicians' desire for cosmetic cost effectiveness has led to the cancellation of Britain's Nimrod AEW, leaving the veteran Shackleton to soldier on until the advent of the American AWACS from 1991.

Fairey Aviation Co Ltd/ Westland Aircraft Ltd.

77

'THE WAY FORWARD TO OPERATION CORPORATE'

By 1980, there had been a partial renaissance of fixed wing in the Fleet Air Arm with the introduction of the Sea Harrier and ski-ramp mini-carriers the first of which, H.M.S. Invincible, had just been handed over to the Royal Navy. These new mini-carriers were really a compromise in design from the anti-carrier lobby of the mid 1960's and although they were very cost effective ships, they were unable to deliver the same punch as the conventional fixed-wing vessels. In particular, there was no provision for any form of airborne early warning, a fact justified at the time with the statement that what was left of the Royal Navy's surface fleet would operate entirely within the NATO context of the Eastern Atlantic. Air defence and AEW would be provided by the Royal Air Force – assuming their shore bases were within sufficient range! The fact that the RAF's airborne early warning system was still in the hands of the piston-engined Shackleton was not stressed by the Government spokesmen at the time.

The new Conservative Government came to office amid a euphoria of alleged increases in defence capability, but as the months passed, the Royal Navy experienced the same uncertainty about its future role as had been the case in 1965. The whole question concerning Britains 'Maritime Strategy' was rudely shattered by the publication of the 1981 Defence White Paper by Defence Secretary John Knott. Ironically titled 'The Way Forward' – a misnomer if there ever was one – the 1981 Defence Review was to achieve the same notoriety as its 1966 predecessor. The number of frigates and destroyers were to be cut by one-third, Invincible was to be sold at a cut down price to the Australians and the Navy's amphibious landing ships 'Fearless' and Intrepid' were to be offered to foreign navies – including Argentina of all places! The cost of the new Trident submarine programme was to be met entirely from the Navy Estimates resulting, amongst other economies, in the proposed withdrawal of the ice-patrol ship 'Endurance' from the South Atlantic. The whole future of the Royal Marines and commitment to reinforce NATO's Northern Flank, or anywhere else, were in doubt.

Events at the other end of the globe were now to take a leading role on the world stage, fortunately before Knotts' cuts started to take effect. Encouraged by the withdrawal of H.M.S. Endurance from the South Atlantic, Argentina now pressed for the 'return' of the Malvinas, eventually leading to the outright invasion of the Falkland Islands and South Georgia on April 2nd 1982. Startled by Argentina's aggression the Government immediately ordered the mobilisation and despatch of a large naval task force to the South Atlantic. The atmosphere of that weekend in Portsmouth Dockyard will never be forgotten and the crowds lining Southsea Front as the Fleet sailed could have been forgiven for their confidence in the Task Force's ability to recapture the Falklands … those with longer memories would recall that the Fleet would be devoid of any airborne early warnings to counter the threat of surface-skimming missiles and aircraft.

The Falklands Conflict and its tragic losses were really the epitome of the misguided political directions to maritime strategy, initiated by the 1965 Defence Review. In the same way as the Beira Patrol in 1966 had forced Mr Healey to demonstrate the value of carrier operations. 'Operation Corporate' completely refuted the text of the 1981 White Paper. The British military response demonstrated the need for naval air power at sea, particularly away from the normal NATO area of operations for the nearest friendly airfield was to be found on Ascension Island, only halfway to the Falklands. As the Task Force pressed southwards, the need for ship-borne airborne early warning was to be highlighted as never before.

The Royal Navy faced a formidable force of Argentinian Mirages, Skyhawks, and Super Etendards, all of which would press home their attacks under shipborne radar cover. The lack of AEW provision initially enabled Argentinian Boeing 707's to monitor the Task Force movements, later compelling the small force of Sea Harriers to fly almost continuous 'CAP' patrols during daylight hours. The British were forced to use valuable ships as radar pickets, away from the main task force, to detect Argentinian air attacks. Tragedy struck on 4th May when H.M.S. Sheffield, in such a role, fell victim to an AM-39 Exocet missile launched by Super Etendards creeping in under Sheffields' Type 996 Radar.

A similar fate befell H.M.S. Coventry on May 25th north of the Falkland Sound when, acting again as an advanced radar picket, she was destroyed by Skyhawk free-fall bombs. Provision of AEW would have enabled the Sea Harriers to have been warned well in advance, thus causing the Skyhawks' destruction or at least diverting them away from their strikes. In the bitter battles over the San Carlos beachhead, Argentinian aircraft were able to use the surrounding hills as a radar 'blank', remaining undetected until almost the moment of attack.

During the Falklands Campaign, a desperate search was made for Double Mamba engines that may have been in storage, even Gannets acting as gate guards having their engines inspected for possible re-use. A check was made on the airworthiness of the surviving Gannets, together with a proposal to use H.M.S. Bulwark in reserve at Portsmouth, as a spare flight deck to operate a few Gannets. Alas, Bulwark's catapults had already been removed and the Gannets could not be operated from Hermes or Invincible due to the ski-ramp. Had the campaign developed into stalemate it is possible that Gannets could have operated from airstrips in South Georgia.

The loss of H.M.S. Sheffield spurred the Government into some belated action to provide AEW cover and the Sea King AEW2 was eventually pressed into service, albeit after the campaign had been drawn to a successful conclusion. Developed in conjunction with Westland and Thorn EMI Electronics, the Sea King AEW2 utilises a Searchwater Radar, a development of the maritime patrol radar found in the Maritime Patrol Nimrod. It is mounted on the starboard side of the helicopter and has to be retracted for landing. In November 1984, 849 Squadron was re-formed and in a reflection of its Gannet days consists of a Headquarters Flight and detached flights aboard Invincible, Ark Royal and Illustrious, to provide an element of airborne early warning again for the Fleet.

Westland Aircraft Limited

'How low can you get?' Roy Morris in exuberant mood, in the process of a low pass at White Waltham.

MAP

Lack of airborne early warning cover in the Falklands conflict was to cause grievous losses to the Royal Navy including to vessels like HMS Sheffield and HMS Coventry, acting as advance radar pickets. A speedy solution was found in the development of the Sea King AEW Mk 2, seen here with its retractable radome. Versatile as the Sea King AEW2 is, the Royal Navy's real requirement must be for a fixed-wing AEW aircraft in the future. All Sea King AEW2's serve with 849 Squadron at Culdrose, maintaining the long link through the Skyraider and Gannet in the provision of the Royal Navy's AEW cover.

PRESERVED GANNETS

An impressive number of Gannets have been preserved around the United Kingdom and it is possible to view examples of most marks of Gannet. The United Kingdom is fortunate in possessing a fine array of aviation museums and in particular, the Fleet Air Arm Museum at Yeovilton, the Imperial War Museum at Duxford, the Cornwall Aero Park at Helston and the Wales Aircraft Museum at Cardiff Airport are well worth a visit in themselves.

GANNET AS1's
XA334   Preserved by the Royal Australian Navy at Camden. New South Wales.
XA434   Preserved by the Royal Australian Navy at Nowra. New South Wales.
XG789   Preserved by the Royal Australian Navy at Moorabin.
AS-00   Preserved outside Surabaya Airport, Indonesia.

GANNET AS4
XA456   Originally at the Fire School at Predannack, Cornwall, now completely destroyed.
XG853   Preserved at Nordholz, West Germany, as UA-113,

GANNET COD-4
XA454   Originally with the Fleet Air Arm Museum then used by the Fire Section at Yeovilton and now probably destroyed.
XA466   Preserved at the Fleet Air Arm Museum Yeovilton, as 777/LM 849 Squadron H.Q. Flight.

GANNET T2
XA508   Originally held at the Royal Naval Engineering College at Manadon, now in the markings 627/GN at the Midland Air Museum at Coventry Airport.

GANNET T5
XG882   Gate guardian at RAF Lossiemouth (originally HMS Fulmar) as 771/LM 849 Squadron H.Q. Flight.
XG883   Originally with the Fleet Air Arm Museum as 773/ BY 849 Squadron H.Q. Flight, now on display at the Wales Aircraft Museum at Cardiff Airport.
XG888   Stored at Lee-on-Solent.
XT752   Stored at Lee-on-Solent, believed to have civilian registration G-APYO.

GANNET ECM6
XG797   Preserved at the Imperial War Museum collection at Duxford, Cambridgeshire, as 766/BY.
XG831   Preserved at the Cornwall Aero Park, Helston.
XA459   Preserved at the Wales Aircraft Museum at Cardiff Airport.

XA460   Preserved at the Kelsterton College of Technology, Flint, North Wales as 768/BY.

GANNET AS6
WN464   Preserved at the Cornwall Aero Park, Helston.

GANNET AEW3
XL449   Preserved at the Wales Aircraft Museum, Cardiff Airport.

XL450   Originally with 431 M.U. at RAF Bruggen, now believed to be scrapped.

XL471   Originally with the Ministry of Defence at Farnborough as 043/R from 849 Squadron 'B' Flight, XL471 is now at Carlisle Airport and privately owned as a source of spares to keep G-BMYP/XL502 airworthy.

XL472   Used for technical training by the Apprentice School at Boscombe Down, now believed to be derelict, as 044/R 849 Squadron 'B' Flight.

XL482   Originally stored at Culdrose, XL482 was test flown in February 1982 with the new registration N1350X and later that month departed for San Antonio, Texas for trials into contra rotating prop-fans by Hamilton Standard who now own the aircraft.

XL497   Gate guardian at HMS Gannet, Prestwick as 041/R 849 Squadron 'B' Flight.

XL500   Originally with the School of Aircraft Handling at Culdrose, then into storage at Lee-on-Solent, XL500 was utilised by Dowty-Rotol noise studies as detailed later.

XL502   At one time used by R.A.E. Bedford for radar trials, XL502 was bought by a British Caledonian pilot and given the civil registration G-BMYP and displayed at several Air Shows during 1987. It was still on the air-show circuit in 1988.

XL503   On display at the Fleet Air Arm Museum Yeovilton as 070/E of 849 Squadron 'D' Flight.

XP226   Originally the gate guard at HMS Dryad, now on display at the Newark Air Museum, Winthorpe, Notts as 073/E of 849 Squadron 'D' Flight.

After Ark Royal's last commission in 1978, it was hoped that an airworthy example could be obtained from the pool of Gannets left at RAF Lossiemouth. Sadly, funds could not be found to allocate a Gannet to the Fleet Air Arm Historic Flight and there is more than a touch of irony in the suggestion that after the Falklands Conflict, an airworthy Gannet AEW3 would not have eased the politicians' embarrassment over the lack of airborne early warning for the Task Force! Three aircraft XG888, XT752 and XL500 were stored in airworthy conditions at Culdrose and occasionally underwent engine runs but it fell to a private company to put a Gannet into the air again early in 1982.

Dowty-Rotol had appreciated that there was a viable market for advanced technology propellers on commuter aircraft, provided that the noise level in the passenger cabin could be reduced. Dowty required to carry out tests on counter-rotating propellers using advanced acoustic measuring equipment. The Gannet proved to be the ideal aircraft to carry out these tests on account of its two four bladed Dowty-Rotol propellers driven by the Double Mamba engine. The characteristic Gannet feature of independently operated propellers proved ideal for this research work. XL500 was assigned to the Dowty tests in Britain, whilst XL482 was re-registered as N1350X and conducted similar trials by Hamilton Standard in the U.S.A.

The Airborne warning equipment was removed from the Gannet and recording and monitoring equipment installed in its place. Noise levels were measured by use of four boom-mounted microphones, projected beyond the propeller to check noise levels in front and behind the aircraft.

Taxying trials were conducted initially with the microphones sited by the runway, followed by flight trials with varied power on each propeller with both engines running. The tests were conducted in collaboration with British Aerospace and Rolls Royce, assisted by Royal Navy personnel.

The Gannets' 30 year old propellors performed perfectly both in the UK and the USA. Test Pilot for the test flying was undertaken by Lt Cdr Lamprey, an ex 849 Squadron member, still current upon Gannets.

Advantage of the tests were taken by show organisers at Yeovilton and Culdrose for their 1984 Air Days to the delight of enthusiasts after which XL500 was placed again in storage at Lee-on-Solent, awaiting further tests if requested.

The end of an era. XL500 flying for Dowty Rotol seen in formation with a Sea King AEW Mk 2 of 849 Squadron over St. Michaels Mount in 1983.

83

COCKPIT INTERIORS - GANNET T5
Typical of T1, T2 and T4

Key to Fig. A

1. Wingfold safety lever.
2. Wingfold selector lever.
3. LP fuel cock lever, starboard.
4. LP fuel cock lever, port.
5. Emergency lighting battery.
6. Outside air temperature gauge.
7. Not used.
8. Harness stowage hook.
9. Weapon sight selector/dimmer control
10. Inoperative.
11. Throttle lever, port engine.
12. Throttle lever, starboard engine.
13. Inoperative.
14. Hydraulic pressure gauge.
15. Oil cooler shutter switches.
16. Fuel recuperator warning indicators.
17. Weapon sight spare filament stowage.
18. Normal inverter failure indicator.
19. Inverter change-over test button.
20. Inverter change-over switch.
21. Triple pressure brake gauge.
22. Ignition warning lights.
23. Emergency flight-fine-pitch-stop switches.
24. Flight-fine-pitch-stop warning light.
25. JPT control switches.
26. Engine synchroniser switch.
27. HP fuel cock lever and relight button, starboard.
28. Aileron trimming switch.
29. Flap selector lever.
30. Wing-locking indicator lights test switch.
31. Rudder trimming control and indicator.
32. RP selector switch.
33. Elevator trimming control and indicator.
34. HP fuel cock lever and relight button, port.
35. Main UHF take-control pushbutton.
36. Main UHF take-control indicator light.
37. Inoperative.
38. Standby UHF pupil/instructor take-control switch.
39. Main UHF controller.
40. Intercomm. power switch (for emergency intercomm.).
41. Parking brake control.

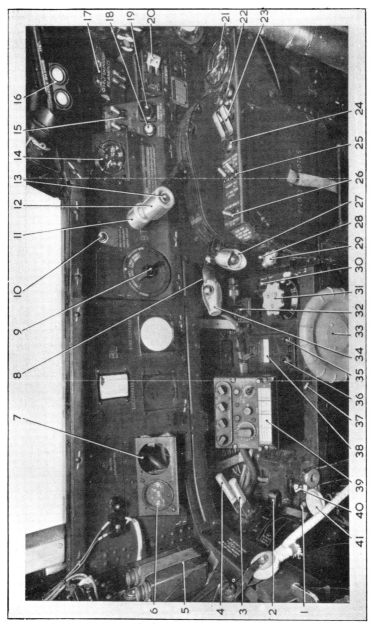

Fig. A.   Front cockpit, Port side.
T Mk. 5

85

Key to Fig. B

1. Fire extinguisher pushbutton, starboard engine.
2. Fire extinguisher pushbutton, engine bay.
3. Fire extinguisher pushbutton, port engine.
4. Taxying lamps switch.
5. Fire warning lights test pushbuttons.
6. Emergency intercomm. switch.
7. UHF mute switch.
8. Bombs/RP selector switch.
9. Undercarriage selector pushbuttons.
10. Pressure head heater override switch.
11. Inoperative.
12. Undercarriage warning light.
13. SHP gauge, port.
14. Weapons sight master switch.
15. Flight instruments power failure indicator.
16. Horizon gyro fast-erection button.
17. Weapon sight.
18. Weapon sight emergency retraction control.
19. SHP gauge, starboard.
20. Inoperative.
21. Dual JPT gauge.
22. JPT warning lights.
23. Pilot's hood jettison control.
24. Generator failure warning lights.
25. Emergency hydraulic selector.
26. Oxygen regulator.
27. Bomb door selector lever.
28. Marker/flare fuzing switch.
29. 2000 lb store selector switch.
30. Arrester hook control lever.
31. Windscreen de-icing pushbutton.
32. Windscreen wiper switch.
33. Fuel transfer indicator, bomb-bay tanks.
34. Emergency accumulator pressure warning indicator.
35. Arrester hook indicator light.
36. Fuel transfer indicators, wing tanks.
37. Engine RPM indicators.
38. Reverse torque indicators.
39. Oil pressure gauge, starboard engine.
40. Compass/DG change-over switch.
41. Oil temperature gauges.
42. Oil pressure gauge, port engine.
43. Radio altimeter.
44. Weapon sight retraction circuit fuse.
45. Fuel contents pushbutton.
46. Fuel contents gauge.
47. Flap position and aileron trim indicator.
48. Pilot's hood control lever.
49. Undercarriage position indicator.
50. Inoperative.

Fig. B.   Front cockpit, Forward view.
T Mk. 5

Key to Fig. C

1. UHF main/standby change-over switch.
2. Standby UHF normal/emergency power switch.
3. Main UHF tone switch.
4. Standby UHF guard/A channel switch.
5. Standby UHF emergency press-to-transmit switch.
6. Cold air control.
7. Starting-fuel pumps master switch.
8. Cold air vent.
9. Inoperative
10. Bomb door indicator.
11. Bomb spacing unit.
12. Bomb jettison pushbutton.
13. Wander lamp.
14. Wander lamp switch.
15. Bomb/fuzing selector.
16. IFF master switch.
17. Emergency stores-jettison switch.
18. Harness stowage fitting.
19. Instrument panel UV lighting dimmer switch.
20. Instrument panel floodlamps dimmer switch.
21. Port side floodlamps dimmer switch.
22. Starboard side floodlamps dimmer switch.
23. Circuit breakers cover-plate.
24. Hood jettison indicator.
25. Flying controls locking lever.
26. Throttles locking lever.
27. Harness go-forward release lever.
28. ZBX controller.
29. Electrical socket for servicing lead.
30. ZBX/UHF audio mixer switch.
31. Switches from outboard inwards:
    2000 lb store master switch
    Inoperative
    Inoperative
    G.45 camera isolating switch
    G.45 camera aperture switch.
32. Hydraulic handpump handle stowage.
33. Battery isolating switch.
34. Switches from outboard inwards:
    Inoperative
    Side panels floodlamps master switch
    Instrument panel floodlamps master switch
    Emergency lamps switch.
35. Pilot's seat adjusting lever.
36. Switches from outboard inwards:
    Navigation lights steady/off/morse switch
    Navigation lights dim/bright switch
    Formation lights steady/off/morse switch
    (Anti-collision on/off switch post mod. 492)
    Formation lights dim/bright switch.
    Identification light steady/off/morse switch.
37. External lights master switch.
38. Hot air control.
39. IFF controller.
40. Engine starter pushbuttons guard switch.
41. Engine starter pushbuttons.
42. Hydraulic handpump.
43. Inoperative

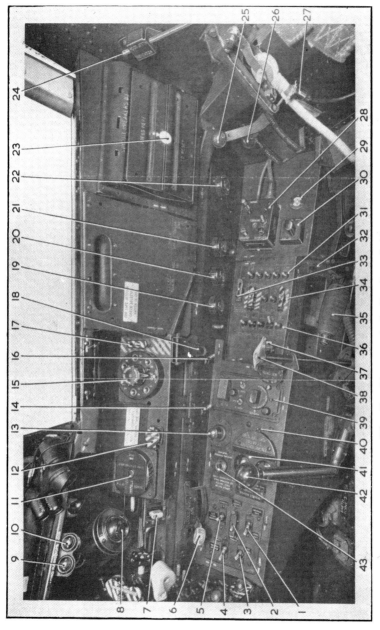

Fig. C.   Front cockpit, Starboard side.
T Mk. 5

Key to Fig. D

1. Standby UHF normal/emergency power switch.
2. Standby UHF guard/A channel switch.
3. Standby UHF emergency press-to-transmit switch.
4. UHF main/standby change-over switch.
5. Main UHF tone switch.
6. Main UHF take-control indicator light.
7. Main UHF take-control pushbutton.
8. Flares/stores selector switch.
9. Inoperative.
10. Markers selector switch.
11. UHF press-to-transmit switch.
12. Smoke float release pushbutton.
13. UHF/ZBX audio switch.
14. Cold air vent.
15. UHF control-column press-to-transmit switch.
16. Armament stores release switch.
17. Inoperative.
18. Throttle lever, port engine.
19. Pilot's Notes and map stowage.
20. Throttle lever, starboard engine.
21. HP fuel cock lever and relight button, starboard.
22. Flap selector lever.
23. HP fuel cock lever and relight button, port.
24. Rudder trimming control.
25. Elevator trimming control.
26. Main UHF controller.
27. Generator reset switches.

90

Fig. D.   Centre cockpit, Port side.
T Mk. 5

91

Key to Fig. E

1. Main UHF mute switch.
2. Ignition warning lights.
3. Emergency intercomm. pushbutton.
4. Engine fire-warning lights.
5. Undercarriage selector lever.
6. Undercarriage position indicator.
7. Fuel contents gauge.
8. Fuel contents gauge change-over switch.
9. Undercarriage warning light.
10. SHP gauge, port.
11. Flight instruments power failure indicator.
12. Horizon gyro fast-erection button.
13. SHP gauge, starboard.
14. Inoperative.
15. Dual JPT gauge.
16. Emergency accumulator pressure warning indicator.
17. JPT warning lights.
18. Generator failure warning lights.
19. Bomb door indicator.
20. Arrester hook warning light.
21. Oxygen regulator.
22. Oil pressure gauge, starboard.
23. Centre-cockpit hood jettison control.
24. RPM indicators.
25. Fuel transfer indicator, bomb bay tanks.
26. Oil temperature gauges.
27. Fuel transfer indicators, wing tanks.
28. Oil pressure gauge, port.
29. Reverse torque indicators.
30. Oil temperature gauges switch.
31. Normal inverter failure indicator.
32. Radio altimeter.
33. Flap position and aileron trim indicator.
34. Flight-fine-pitch-stops warning light.
35. Emergency flight-fine-pitch-stop switches.

Fig. E.   Centre cockpit, Forward view.
T Mk. 5

Key to Fig. F

1. Cold air control.
2. UV lights dimmer switch.
3. Instrument panel floodlamps master switch.
4. Electrical socket for servicing lead.
5. Fuel pump test switch and socket.
6. Instrument panel floodlamps dimmer switch.
7. Side panel floodlamps dimmer switch.
8. Emergency lighting switch.
9. Wander lamp switch.
10. Circuit breaker, ARI.5848 inverter supply.
11. Circuit breakers, busbars supply.
12. Harness go-forward release lever.
13. Hood lock release handle.
14. Harness stowage fitting.
15. Wander lamp.
16. Side panel floodlamps master switch.

Fig. F. Centre cockpit, Starboard side.
T Mk. 5

95

COCKPIT INTERIORS - GANNET AEW3

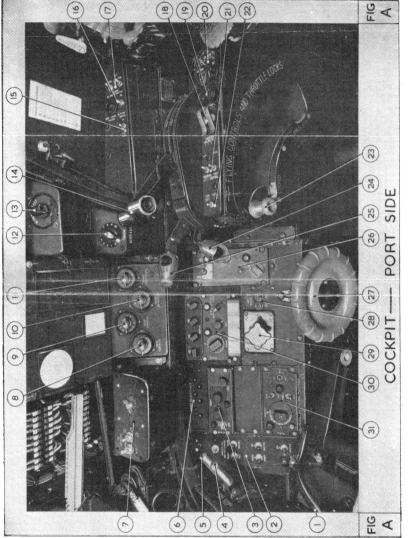

Cockpit, Port Side
AEW Mk 3

97

Key to Fig. B

1. Flap position indicator
2. I/C lock switch
3. TACAN aerial switch
4. Undercarriage selector buttons
5. Emergency lights switch
6. Pilot's hood control lever
7. Arrester hook lever
8. Aileron trim indicator
9. Engine emergency rating switch
10. Rudder trim indicator
11. Hood jettison lever
12. Nose wheel doors indicator
13. Radio altimeter limit lights
14. Centralised warning system light
15. Fuel filter icing indicator
16. Centralised warning system light
17. Airframe de-icing indicator
18. Engine power indicators
19. J.P.T. indicators
20. Wing fold latch pin indicator
21. Auto-pilot indicator
22. Oxygen remote blinker
23. R.P.M. indicators
24. Fuel contents gauge
25. Fuel contents selector switch
26. Fuel transfer indicator lights
27. Windscreen de-icing indicator
28. Fuel transfer lights test button
29. Windscreen de-icing circuit-breaker
30. Centralised warning system sound circuit-breaker
31. Fuel flowmeter re-set button
32. Wander light (deleted in later aircraft)
33. Fuel flowmeter
34. Oil temperature gauges
35. Oil pressure gauges
36. Turn-and-slip stand-by switch
37. Compass/D.G. switch
38. TACAN indicator
39. Radio altimeter indicator
40. Flap selector lever
41. Flap emergency selector switch
42. Undercarriage position indicator
43. Hydraulic pressure gauge

COCKPIT—FORWARD VIEW

Cockpit, Forward view
AEW Mk3

FIG B

FIG B

A.L. MAY 1961

99

1 Chart board and Pilot's Notes stowage
2 Engine bay fire-extinguisher button
3 Recuperator warning indicators
4 Fire.warning test button
5 Centralised warning indicator
6 Ventilation louvre
7 Switch panel (see inset)
8 Harness stowage lug
9 Alternator failure indicators
10 DC failure indicators
11 Reverse torque ind cators
12 Ventilation master switches
13 Switch panel (see inset)
14 OAT gauge
15 Ground test connection
16 Ground test connection
17 Hood jettison indicator
18 Arrester hook emergency lever
19 Undercarriage emergency lever
20 Flaps emergencv lever
21 Wing fold selector lever
22 Wing fold safety lever
23 AVS selector
24 Circuit-breaker panel
25 Emergency accumulator re-charge knob
26 Emergency accumulator pressure gauge
27 Oxygen regulator
28 Airframe de-icing interval selector
29 Seat adjusting lever
30 Oxygen contents gauge
31 Cold air control
32 Hot air control
33 Auto-pilot controller

◄NOTE—Post Mod 716, the switching on item C13 is arranged as
follows, reading from left to right, top to bottom:—

E2B Normal-off-emergency switch
Two power reset switches
Formation on-off switch
Navigation dim-bright and steady-flash switches
Battery master switch
Cockpit and external lighting switches ►

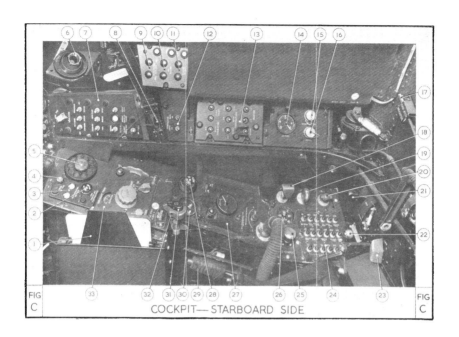

FIG C

COCKPIT— STARBOARD SIDE

FIG C

Switch panel (Item 7 of Fig C)

Switch panel (Item 13 of Fig C)

MODELLERS SECTION

The following series of photographs have been included to help anyone modelling a Gannet. They show close-up details of the fuselage, undercarriage and nosewheel handling trolly and wing-hinges. Also included is a sequence showing the wings unfolding into flying readiness.

105

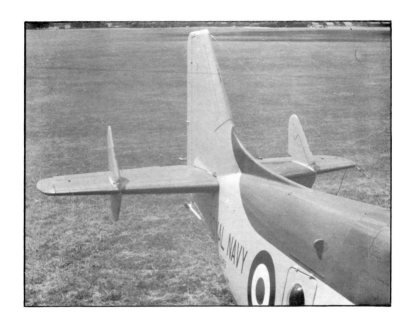

LEADING PARTICULARS

GANNET AS1

Span	54.33 ft (16.6m)	
Length	43 ft. (13.1m)	
Height	13.71 ft. (4.18m)	
Wing Area	482.8 sq.ft. (44.9 sq.m)	

POWERPLANT
1 x Armstrong Siddeley Double
Mamba 100 turboshaft

WEIGHTS
Empty weight 15,069 lb.
All-up weight 19,600 lb.

PERFORMANCE
Maximum Speed	270 knots
Cruising Speed	190 knots
Range	600 nautical miles
Endurance	4-5 hours
Ceiling	25,000 ft.

STORES
16 x 3 inch rocket projectiles
2 x A.S.W. torpedoes or mines
Depth charges
Ferranti ASV radar retractable radome

GANNET AS4

Span, Length, Height – *As Gannet AS1*

POWERPLANT
1 x Armstrong Siddeley Double
Mamba 101 turboshaft

WEIGHTS
Empty weight 14,069 lb.
All-up weight 23,446 lb.

PERFORMANCE
Maximum Speed	260 knots
Cruising Speed	130 knots
Range	575 nautical miles
Endurance	4.9 hours
Ceiling	25,000 ft.

STORES
As Gannet AS1

GANNET AEW3

Span	54.33 ft (16.6m)
Length	44 ft. (13.4m)
Height	16.83 ft. (5.13m)
Wing Area	490 sq.ft. (42.7 sq.m)

POWERPLANT
1 x Double Mamba 102

WEIGHTS
All-up weight 25,000 lb.

PERFORMANCE
Maximum Speed	217 knots
Cruising Speed	175 knots
Range	700 nautical miles
Endurance	6 hours
Ceiling	25,000 ft.

STORES
AN / APS 20E Radar

GANNET DEVELOPMENT AIRCRAFT

VR 546	(F 8270)	1st Prototype	1
VR 557	(F 8271)	2nd Prototype	1
VR 488	(F 8749)	3rd Prototype	1

GANNET PRODUCTION

WN 339 - WN 364	(F 9111 - 9136)	A.S. MK 1	26
WN 365	(F 9137)	T. MK 2 (Prototype)	1
WN 366 - WN 378	(F 9138 - 9150)	A.S. MK 1	13
WN 390 - WN 429	(F 9151 - 9190)	A.S. MK 1	40
WN 445 - WN 464	(F 9191 - 9210)	A.S. MK 1	20
XA 319 - XA 364	(F 9211 - 9256)	A.S. MK 1	46
XA 387 - XA 409	(F 9257 - 9279)	A.S. MK 1	23
XA 410 - XA 433	(F 9280 - 9303)	A.S. MK 4	24
XA 434	(F 9304)	A.S. MK 1	1
XA 435	(F 9305)	A.S. MK 4	1
XA 436	(F 9306)	A.S. MK 1	1
XA 454 - XA 473	(F 9307 - 9326)	A.S. MK 4	20
XD 898	(F 9327)	A.S. MK 1	1
XA 508 - XA 530	(F 9328 - 9350)	T. MK 2	23
XG 783 - XG 798	(F 9351 - 9366)	A.S. MK 4	16
XG 825 - XG 826	(F 9367 - 9368)	A.S. MK 1	2
XG 827 - XG 836	(F 9369 - 9378)	A.S. MK 4	10
XG 839 - XG 840	(F 9381 - 9382)	A.S. MK 4	2
XG 843 - XG 844	(F 9385 - 9386)	A.S. MK 4	2
XG 846	(F 9388)	A.S. MK 4	1
XG 848 - XG 850	(F 9390 - 9392)	A.S. MK 4	3
XG 852 - XG 853	(F 9394 - 9395)	A.S. MK 4	2
XG 869 - XG 881	(F 9398 - 9410)	T. MK 2	13
XG 882 - XG 887	(F 9411 - 9416)	T. MK 5	6
XG 888	(F 9417)	T. MK 2	1
XG 889 - XG 890	(F 9418 - 9419)	T. MK 5	2
XJ 440	(F 9431)	A.E.W. MK 3 (Prototype)	1
XL 449 - XL 456	(F 9432 - 9439)	A.E.W. MK 3	8
XL 471 - XL 482	(F 9440 - 9451)	A.E.W. MK 3	12
XL 493 - XL 503	(F 9452 - 9462)	A.E.W. MK 3	11
XP 197 - XP 199	(F 9463 - 9465)	A.E.W. MK 3	3
XP 224 - XP 229	(F 9466 - 9471)	A.E.W. MK 3	6
XR 431 - XR 433	(F 9514 - 9516)	A.E.W. MK 3	3

PRODUCTION QUANTITIES (Including Prototypes)

Gannet A.S. MK 1		176
Gannet T. MK 2		38
Gannet A.E.W. MK 3		44
Gannet A.S. MK 4		81
Gannet T. MK 5		8
	Total	347

The Gannets supplied to the Royal Navy as C.O.D. MK 4 or E.C.M. MK 6 were modified from the above aircraft, as also were those supplied to the following overseas customers:

Royal Australian Navy	33 A.S. MK 1 and 3 T. MK 2
Federal German Navy	15 A.S. MK 1 and 1 T. MK 5
Indonesian Navy	16 A.S. MK 4 and 2 T. MK 5

114

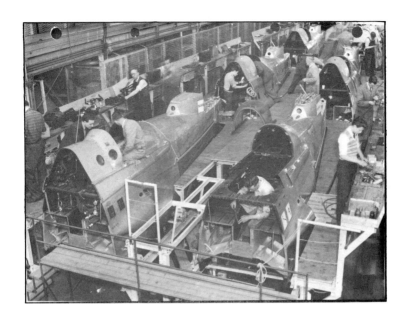

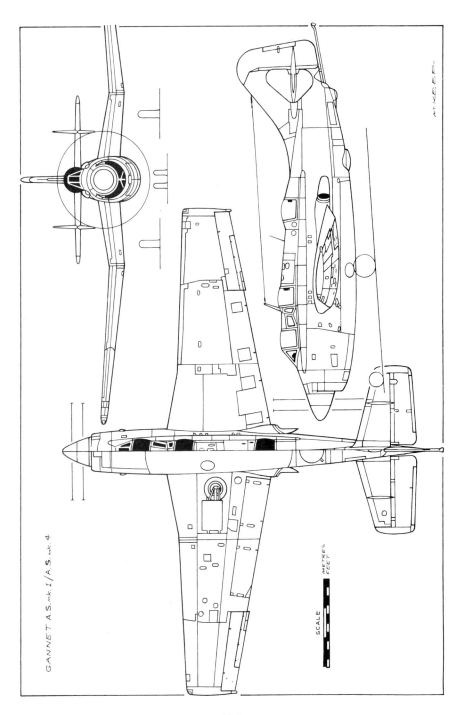

GANNET A.S.mk 1 / A.S.mk 4

SCALE
METRES
FEET

M.KEEP.

116

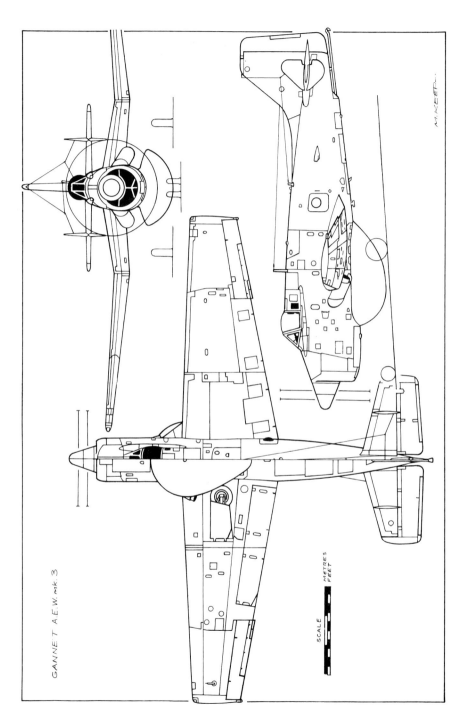

GANNET A.E.W. mk 3

SCALE
METRES
FEET

M.KEEP

117

Fairey Gannet camouflage and markings

FAIREY GANNET COLOUR KEY

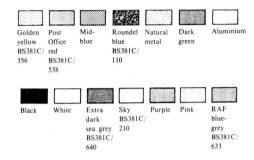

Golden	Post	Mid-	Roundel	Natural	Dark	Aluminium
yellow	Office	blue	blue	metal	green	
BS381C/	red		BS381C/			
356	BS381C/		110			
	538					

Black	White	Extra	Sky	Purple	Pink	RAF
		dark	BS381C/			blue-
		sea grey	210			grey
		BS381C/				BS381C/
		640				633

DRAWINGS BY MIKE KEEP

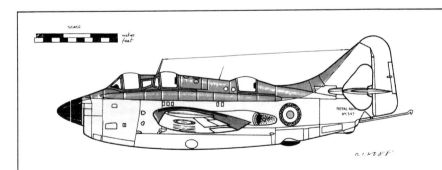

Fairey Gannet AS.1 WN347 of No.703X NAS in 1954. Top surfaces are Extra dark sea grey, lower surfaces Sky. Lettering, serials and spinners black. Codes were not carried.

118

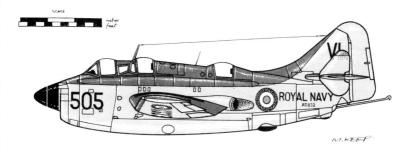

Fairey Gannet AS.4 XG832/505-VL of No. 700G NAS based at Yeovilton in 1959. Extra dark sea grey and Sky with mid-blue finlet tips. Spinners, serials, codes and lettering black.

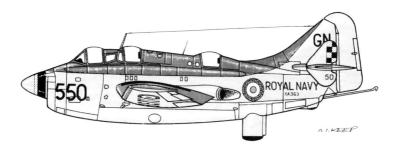

Fairey Gannet AS.1 XA363/550-GN of 719 NAS flying from Eglinton in the late 1950's. Extra dark sea grey and Sky finish with serials, codes and lettering black. Spinners and outer finlet checks are yellow and black.

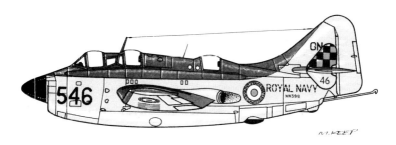

Fairey Gannet AS.1 WN398/546-GN of 719 NAS, Eglinton. Extra dark sea grey and Sky colouring with black spinners, serials, codes and lettering. Revised finlet colours are red and black.

119

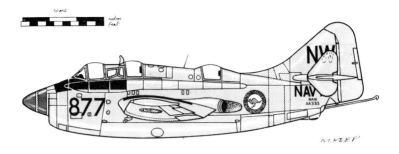

Fairey Gannet T.2 XA333/877-NW of No. 724 Squadron, Royal Australian Navy based at Nowra in 1963. Aluminium dope overall with Golden yellow training bands. Spinners are believed to be green and yellow. Anti-glare panel and other markings are black.

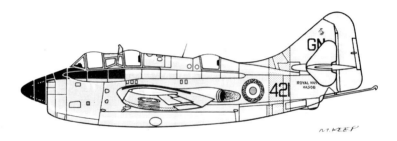

Fairey Gannet T.2 XA508/421-GN of 737 NAS was based at Eglinton in 1955. Overall painted aluminium finish with Golden yellow training bands. Spinners, anti-glare panel and other markings are black. Squadron crest above tail code.

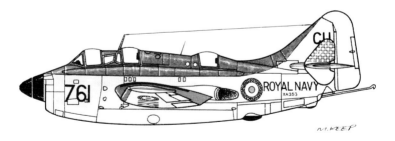

Fairey Gannet AS.1 XA353/761-CU of 796 NAS based at Culdrose 1957-58. Finish is Extra dark sea grey and Sky. Spinner, codes, lettering and serial numbers are black. Outer finlet colours are red and white.

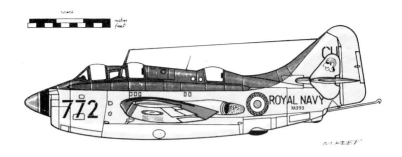

Fairey Gannet AS.1 XA393/772-CU of 796 NAS, Culdrose, 1958. Standard finish with red, silver and black spinners. Pirate on finlets (faces forward on both sides) is thought to be pink, red and black with white teeth and black detail.

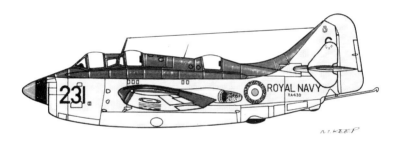

Fairey Gannet AS.4 XA430/231-C of 810 NAS aboard HMS *Centaur* in 1959. Extra dark sea grey and Sky finish with red and black spinners. Serials, codes and lettering black. Squadron crest on fin. Red flashes were applied to finlets in 1960.

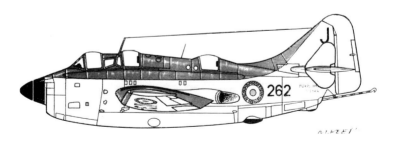

Fairey Gannet AS.1 WN346/262-J of 812 NAS embarked in HMS *Eagle* during 1956. Standard FAA finish of Extra dark sea grey top and Sky lower surfaces. '62' in black on white panel on wing leading edges. Spinner and all remaining markings black.

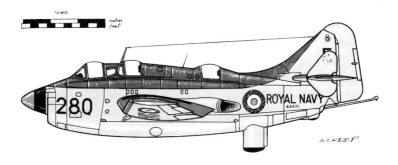

Fairey Gannet AS.4 XA471/280-E of 814 NAS in HMS *Eagle* circa 1958. Extra dark sea grey and Sky colouring with mid-blue and black spinners. Unit crest on fin. '80' in white on wing leading edges. All other markings black.

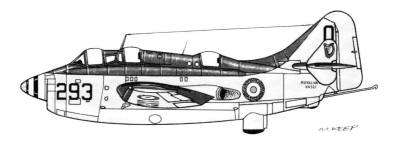

Fairey Gannet AS.1 XA321/293-O of 815 NAS in HMS *Ark Royal* in 1956. Extra dark sea grey and Sky finish with red, black and white spinners. Codes, serials and lettering are black. Note the unit's dark green and yellow harp motif on the outer finlets.

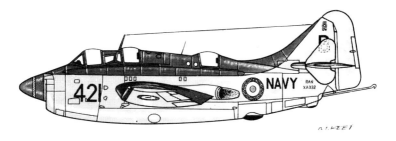

Fairey Gannet AS.1 XA332/421-B of No. 816 Squadron, Royal Australian Navy operating from HMAS *Melbourne* during 1955. Standard Royal Navy finish with green and yellow spinners. Codes, serials and lettering black. Unit crest on fin tip.

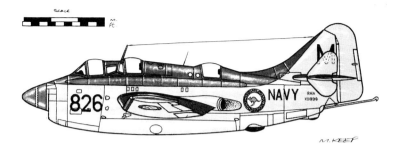

Fairey Gannet AS.1 XD898/M-826 of No.816 Squadron Royal Australian Navy operating from HMAS *Melbourne* during 1961-62. FAA finish with black codes, lettering and serials. Spinners are green and yellow. Note that Kangaroo feet on wing roundels face aircraft centre-line.

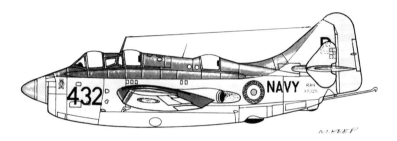

Fairey Gannet AS.1 XA326/432-B of No.817 Squadron, Royal Australian Navy in HMAS *Melbourne* in 1955-56. Standard overall colouring with black serials, lettering and codes. Checks on outer finlets are thought to be red and yellow, spinners also being in these colours. Squadron crest on nose.

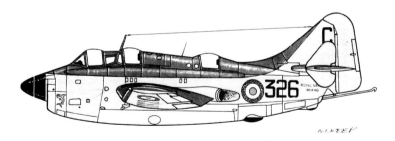

Fairey Gannet AS.1 WN448/326-C of 820 NAS aboard HMS *Centaur* in 1956. Extra dark sea grey and Sky with black spinners. codes, lettering and serials. Shark on nose is bright blue and white with red mouth. Outlines and details are black.

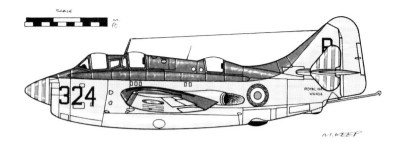

Fairey Gannet AS.1 WN404/324-B of 820 NAS in HMS *Bulwark* during 1956-57. Extra dark sea grey and Sky finish with purple and white spinners and finlets. Remaining markings are black.

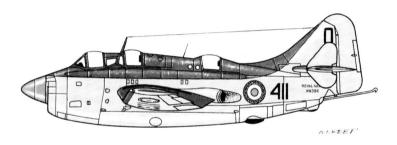

Fairey Gannet AS.1 WN396/411-O of 824 NAS in HMS *Ark Royal* in 1955. Extra dark sea grey and Sky finish with red spinners. Codes, serials and lettering black.

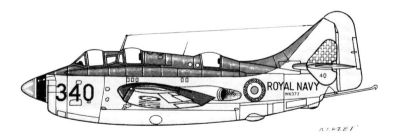

Fairey Gannet AS.1 WN377/340 of 825 NAS in 1957. Standard FAA finish with red, white and black spinners and red and white outer finlets. All other markings are black.

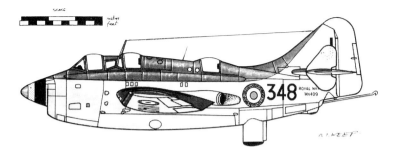

Fairey Gannet AS.1 WN409/348-J of 826 NAS in HMS *Eagle* during 1955. Extra dark sea grey and Sky colouring with red, yellow and black spinners. Lettering, serials and codes are black. '48' on wing leading edges is white.

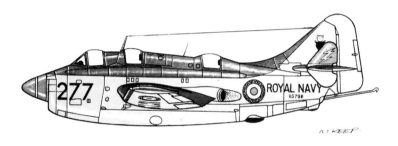

Fairey Gannet ECM.6 XG798/277 of 831 NAS at Culdrose during 1961. Standard colouring with red and yellow spinners and outer finlets. Inner finlets are red only. 'Flook' character on fin is black and white. Remaining markings are black.

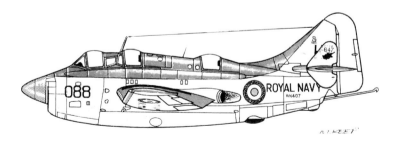

Fairey Gannet AS.1 WN407/088-HF of 847 NAS at Cyprus in 1957-58. Standard finish with black map of Cyprus on finlets. Spinners and '847' are thought to be blue. Squadron crest on fin. Codes and lettering black. Note black '88' on white wing leading edge panel.

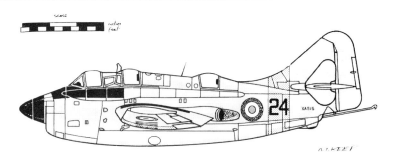

Fairey Gannet T.2 XA515/24 of Empire Test Pilots School at Farnborough. Painted aluminium and Golden yellow finish with remaining trim in black.

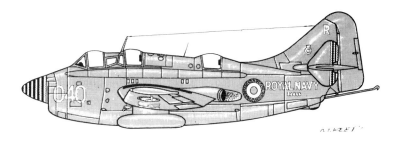

Fairey Gannet COD.4 XA466/040-R of 'B' Flight, 849 NAS aboard HMS *Ark Royal* in 1972. RAF blue-grey overall with black and yellow spinner and finlet stripes. Unit crest on fin. Remaining markings are white.

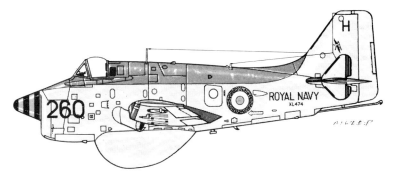

Fairey Gannet AEW.3 XL474/260-H of 'A' Flight, 849 NAS in HMS *Hermes* in 1969. Extra dark sea grey and Sky finish with red and black spinners and finlet stripes. Black and white Albatross upon a red 'A' on fin. All other markings are black.

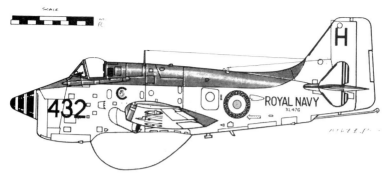

Fairey Gannet AEW.3 XL476/432-H of 'C' Flight, 849 NAS embarked in HMS *Hermes* during 1960. Standard FAA finish with black and white spinners and finlet stripes. Remaining markings are black. Note squadron crest within 'C' on fuselage.

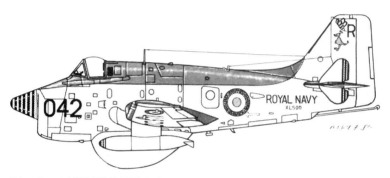

Fairey Gannet AEW.3 XL500/042-R of 'B' Flight, 849 NAS aboard HMS *Ark Royal* in 1973. Standard finish with black and yellow spinners, tank tips, finlet stripes and Bee on tail. Other fin marking is a red, crowned Dragon. Codes, serials and lettering are black.

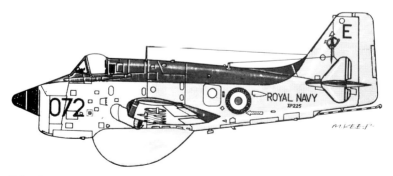

Fairey Gannet AEW.3 XP225/072-E of 'D' Flight, 849 NAS aboard HMS *Eagle*. Standard finish with dark blue and white spinner and finlet stripes. Chinese character on tail is red. All other markings are black.

Production Credits

Typesetting	Patti Palmer
Design	Adrian Hillier
Layout	Helen Tobin
Printer	Darren Hall
Paper	Alliance
Binding	West Country Binders
Drawings	Mike Keep
	(Scale aircraft modelling)
Photographic &	Fred Ballam
Artwork Assistance	Ray Sturtivant
Conception	Brian Fiddler
	David Gibbings
	David Picton-Phillips

NOTES

NOTES

NOTES

NOTES